Wonders

On Track
for PARCC Assessments

Unit
Assessments

Mc
Graw
Hill
Education

www.mheonline.com/readingwonders

Mc
Graw
Hill
Education

Send all inquiries to:
McGraw-Hill Education
Two Penn Plaza
New York, New York 10121

ISBN: 978-0-02-131365-5
MHID: 0-02-131365-2

Printed in the United States of America.

1 2 3 4 5 6 7 8 9 QVS 20 19 18 17 16 15
                    A

Table of Contents

Teacher Introduction

On Track for PARCC Assessments Unit Assessments

The *On Track for PARCC Assessments Unit Assessments* component is an integral part of the complete assessment program aligned with *Reading Wonders* and the Common Core State Standards (CCSS).

Purpose

This component reports on the outcome of student learning. As students complete each unit of the reading program, they will be assessed on their understanding of key instructional content and their ability to write to source texts/stimuli. The results serve as a summative assessment by providing a status of current achievement in relation to student progress through the CCSS-aligned curriculum. The results of the assessments can be used to inform subsequent instruction, aid in making leveling and grouping decisions, and point toward areas in need of reteaching or remediation.

Focus

On Track for PARCC Assessments Unit Assessments focuses on key areas of English Language Arts as identified by the CCSS—comprehension of literature and informational text, vocabulary acquisition and use, command of the conventions of the English language, and genre writing in response to sources.

Each unit assessment also provides students familiarity with the item types, the test approaches, and the increased rigor associated with the *Partnership for Assessment of Readiness for College and Careers* (PARCC) summative assessment system.

Test Administration

Each unit assessment should be administered once the instruction for the specific unit is completed. Make copies of the unit assessment for the class. You will need copies of the Answer Key pages that feature the scoring tables for each student taking the assessment. These tables provide a place to list student scores. The data from each unit assessment charts student progress and underscores strengths and weaknesses.

This component is the pencil-and-paper version of the assessment. You can administer the online version of the test, which allows for tech-enhanced item functionality.

NOTE: Due to time constraints, you may wish to administer the unit assessment over multiple days. For example, students can complete Questions 1–25 on the first day and complete the Performance-Based Assessment task on another. For planning purposes, the recommended time for each task is 60 minutes for the Narrative Writing task, 90 minutes for the Research Simulation task, and 75 minutes for the Literary Analysis task. If you decide to break up administration by assessment sections, please remember to withhold those sections of the test students are not completing to ensure test validity.

Item #15 in each assessment is focused on students comparing texts/writing across texts. This is a continuation of the optional activity featured in the *Weekly Assessments,* and it provides valuable practice for the type of critical thinking and writing required in the Performance-Based Assessment tasks. If you feel the tasks give your students adequate exposure to this type of writing and want to reduce test administration time, you can decide not to administer item #15 and remove that page from the test packet. Deleting the item will result in a 38-point skill test; note this deletion in your scoring tables.

After each student has a copy of the assessment, provide a version of the following directions:

Say: *Write your name and the date on the question pages for this assessment.* (When students are finished, continue with the directions.) *You will read four texts and answer questions about them. In the next part of the test, you will read drafts and/or passages that you will revise or edit for the correct grammar, mechanics, and usage. In the final part of the test, you will read sources, answer questions about them, and write a response based on the assignment you will find, which will ask you to use those sources in your writing.*

Read each part of the test carefully. For multiple-choice items, completely fill in the circle next to the correct answer or answers. For items that ask you to write on the page, look carefully at the directions to answer the question. You may be asked to match items, circle or underline choices, complete a chart, or place details in order. For constructed response items, write your response on the lines provided. For the performance-based task, write your response on a clean sheet of paper. When you have completed the assessment, put your pencil down and turn the pages over. You may begin now.

Answer procedural questions during the assessment, but do not provide any assistance on the items or selections. Have extra paper on hand for students to use for their task responses. After the class has completed the assessment, ask students to verify that their names and the date are written on the necessary pages.

Assessment Items

Unit assessments feature the following item types—selected response (SR), multiple selected response (MSR), evidence-based selected response (EBSR), constructed response (CR), technology-enhanced constructed response (TECR), and extended constructed response (ECR). (Please note that print-adapted versions of TECR items are available in this component; the full functionality of the items is available only through the online assessment.) This variety of item types provides multiple methods of assessing student understanding, allows for deeper investigation into skills and strategies, and provides students an opportunity to become familiar with the kinds of questions they will encounter in PARCC assessments.

Performance-Based Assessments

Each unit features a Performance-Based Assessment (PBA) task. Students will complete two examples of each type featured in PARCC by the end of the year.

The task types are:

- **Narrative Writing:** Students use a short piece of fiction as a starting point to write their own story, which may further explore the events or reimagine the point of view of the original.
- **Research Simulation:** Students explore an informational topic presented through three articles and/or multimedia stimuli and synthesize information to write their own analytic essay.
- **Literary Analysis:** Students read two pieces of literature closely to write an analytic essay that connects the two sources.

The PBAs assess standards that address comprehension, genre writing, and the use of standard English language conventions (ELC). The stimulus texts and questions in each task build toward the goal of the final writing topic.

Overview

- Students will read four texts in each assessment and respond to items focusing on comprehension skills and vocabulary strategies. These items assess the ability to access meaning from close reading of the texts and demonstrate understanding of unknown and multiple-meaning words and phrases.
- Students will then read a draft that requires corrections to or clarifications of its use of the conventions of standard English language and/or complete a cloze passage that requires correct usage identification.
- Students are then presented with a Performance-Based Assessment task.

Each test item in *On Track for PARCC Assessments Unit Assessments* (as well as in weekly and benchmark assessments) has a Depth of Knowledge (DOK) level assigned to it.

DOK 1 involves using word parts (affixes, roots, and so on) to determine the meaning of an unknown word or non-contextual items assessing synonym/antonym and multiple-meaning words; identifying/locating information in the text; editing to fix errors.

DOK 2 involves using context to determine the meaning of an unknown word and dealing with figurative language in context; analyzing text structures/story elements; revising writing.

DOK 3 involves making inferences using text evidence and analyzing author's craft.

DOK 4 involves using multiple stimulus texts and writing across texts; writing an essay in response to stimulus text(s).

The four reading selections are "cold reads" that reflect the unit theme to support the focus of the classroom instruction. Texts fall within the Lexile band 925L–1070L. Complexity on this quantitative measure grows throughout the units, unless a qualitative measure supports text placement outside a lockstep Lexile continuum.

Comprehension

Comprehension items assess student understanding of the text through the use of the Comprehension Skills, Literary Elements, and Text Features taught in each unit.

Vocabulary

Vocabulary items ask students to demonstrate the ability to uncover the meanings of unknown and multiple-meaning words and phrases using Vocabulary Strategies.

English Language Conventions

Ten items in each unit ask students to demonstrate their command of the conventions of standard English.

Performance-Based Assessment

Students complete one task per unit, the final result being a written product in the specified task genre.

Scoring

Use the scoring tables to assign final unit assessment scores. Each vocabulary and comprehension item is worth 2 points. Give partial credit of 1 point for an EBSR where Part A is correct but Part B is incorrect or only partially correct. MSR and TECR items should be answered correctly in full, though you may choose to provide partial credit. Each ELC item is worth 1 point.

For CR and ECR items, use the correct response parameters provided in the Answer Key and the scoring rubrics below to assign a score. Responses that show a complete lack of understanding or are left blank should be given a 0.

CONSTRUCTED RESPONSE SCORING RUBRIC

2	• well-crafted and concise, showing thorough understanding of underlying skill • uses appropriate text evidence
1	• shows partial understanding of underlying skill • uses text evidence, but examples are too general

EXTENDED CONSTRUCTED RESPONSE SCORING RUBRIC

4	• shows understanding of question and uses appropriate text evidence • provides acceptably complete answer to question • organization of response is meaningful • stays on topic; ideas are linked to one another with effective transitions • has correct spelling, grammar, usage, and mechanics
3	• shows understanding of question and uses appropriate text evidence • provides somewhat complete answer to question • organization is somewhat meaningful • maintains focus; ideas are linked to one another • has occasional errors in spelling, grammar, usage, and mechanics
2	• shows partial understanding of question and uses some appropriate text evidence • provides incomplete answer to question • organization is weak • writing is careless; contains extraneous information and ineffective transitions • requires effort to read easily • has noticeable errors in spelling, grammar, usage, and mechanics
1	• shows minimal understanding of question and uses little to no appropriate text evidence • provides barely acceptable answer to question • lacks organization • writing is erratic with little focus; ideas are not connected to each other • is difficult to follow • has frequent errors in spelling, grammar, usage, and mechanics

Score each PBA Prose Constructed Response (PCR) holistically, using the rubrics that follow. Literary Analysis and Research Simulation PCRs are scored on a 19-point scale: 4 points for reading comprehension (RC), 12 points for written expression (WE), and 3 points for English language conventions (LC). Narrative Writing PCRs are scored on a 15-point scale: 12 points for written expression (WE) and 3 points for English language conventions (LC).

Unscorable PCRs are unrelated to the topic, illegible, contain little or no writing, or show little to no command of the conventions of standard English.

A top-line anchor paper response is included with the PBA Answer Key to assist with scoring.

SCORING RUBRIC: NARRATIVE WRITING TASK

Score Point	Narrative Elements	Writing: Written Expression	Writing: Knowledge of Language & Conventions
4		• is **effectively** developed with narrative elements and is **consistently task-appropriate** • demonstrates **purposeful** coherence, clarity, and cohesion that make it **easy to follow** progression of ideas • establishes and maintains **effective** style, attending to discipline's norms and conventions	n/a
3	May include, as appropriate: • establishing situation • establishing context • situating events in time and place • organizing logical sequence of events • describing scenes, objects, or people • developing characters and their personalities • developing point of view • developing characters' motives • using dialogue	• is **mostly effectively** developed with narrative elements and is **mostly task-appropriate** • demonstrates coherence, clarity, and cohesion that make it **fairly easy to follow** progression of ideas • establishes and maintains **mostly effective** style, attending to discipline's norms and conventions	• demonstrates **full command** of standard English conventions at appropriate level of complexity • may have a **few minor errors** in grammar, mechanics, and usage, but **meaning is clear**
2		• is developed with **some** narrative elements and is **somewhat task-appropriate** • demonstrates **some** coherence, clarity, and/or cohesion that make progression of ideas **usually discernable but not obvious** • has **somewhat effective** style, **generally** attending to discipline's norms and conventions	• demonstrates **some command** of standard English conventions at appropriate level of complexity • **may** have errors in grammar, mechanics, and usage that **occasionally impede understanding,** but **meaning is generally clear**
1		• is **minimally** developed with **few** narrative elements and is **limited in its task-appropriateness** • demonstrates **limited** coherence, clarity, and/or cohesion that make progression of ideas **somewhat unclear** • has style with **limited** effectiveness, with **limited** awareness of discipline's norms	• demonstrates **limited command** of standard English conventions at appropriate level of complexity • **may** have errors in grammar, mechanics, and usage that **often impede understanding**
0		• is **undeveloped** and/or **inappropriate** to task • lacks coherence, clarity, and cohesion • has **inappropriate** style with **little to no** awareness of discipline's norms	• demonstrates **no command** of standard English conventions • **frequent and varied errors** in grammar, mechanics, and usage **impede understanding**

SCORING RUBRIC: LITERARY ANALYSIS and RESEARCH SIMULATION TASKS

Score Point	Reading: Comprehension of Key Ideas & Details	Writing: Written Expression	Writing: Knowledge of Language & Conventions
4	• demonstrates **full comprehension** of ideas stated explicitly and inferentially • provides **accurate** analysis • supports analysis with **effective** text evidence	• addresses prompt and provides **effective and comprehensive** development of claim or topic that is **consistently task-appropriate**, using **clear and convincing** reasoning and **relevant text** evidence • demonstrates **purposeful** coherence, clarity, and cohesion that make it **easy to follow** progression of ideas • establishes and maintains **effective** style, attending to discipline's norms and conventions	n/a
3	• demonstrates **comprehension** of ideas stated explicitly and/or inferentially • provides **mostly accurate** analysis • supports analysis with **adequate** text evidence	• addresses prompt and provides **mostly effective** development of claim or topic that **is mostly task-appropriate**, using **clear** reasoning and **relevant text** evidence • demonstrates coherence, clarity, and cohesion that make it **fairly easy to follow** progression of ideas • establishes and maintains **mostly effective** style, attending to discipline's norms and conventions	• demonstrates **full command** of standard English conventions at appropriate level of complexity • may have a **few minor errors** in grammar, mechanics, and usage, but **meaning is clear**
2	• demonstrates **basic comprehension** of ideas stated explicitly and/or inferentially • provides **generally accurate** analysis • supports analysis with **basic** text evidence	• addresses prompt and provides **some** development of claim or topic that **is generally task-appropriate**, using **some** reasoning and **text-based** evidence • demonstrates **some** coherence, clarity, and/or cohesion that make progression of ideas **usually discernable but not obvious** • has **somewhat effective** style, **generally** attending to discipline's norms and conventions	• demonstrates **some command** of standard English conventions at appropriate level of complexity • **may** have errors in grammar, mechanics, and usage that **occasionally impede understanding**, but **meaning is generally clear**
1	• demonstrates **limited comprehension** of ideas • provides **minimally accurate** analysis • supports analysis with **limited** text evidence	• addresses prompt and provides **minimal** development of claim or topic that is **limited in its task-appropriateness**, using **limited** reasoning and **text-based** evidence *OR* developed, text-based response shows **little or no awareness** of prompt • demonstrates **limited** coherence, clarity, and/or cohesion that make progression of idea **somewhat unclear** • has style with **limited** effectiveness, with **limited** awareness of discipline's norms	• demonstrates **limited command** of standard English conventions at appropriate level of complexity • **may** have errors in grammar, mechanics, and usage that **often impede understanding**
0	• demonstrates **no comprehension** of ideas • provides **inaccurate or no** analysis • supports analysis with **little to no** text evidence	• is **undeveloped** and/or **inappropriate** to task • **lacks** coherence, clarity, and cohesion • has **inappropriate** style with **little to no** awareness of discipline's norms	• demonstrates **no command** of standard English conventions • **frequent and varied errors** in grammar, mechanics, and usage **impede understanding**

Evaluating Scores

Unit Assessments

The goal of each unit assessment is to evaluate student mastery of previously taught material. The expectation is for students to score 80% or higher on the assessment as a whole.

Within this score, the expectation is for students to score 75% or higher on each section of the assessment.

For students who do not meet these benchmarks, assign appropriate lessons from the Tier 2 online PDFs. Refer to the summative assessment pages in the Teacher's Edition of *Reading Wonders* for specific lessons.

The Answer Keys have been constructed to provide the information you need to aid your understanding of student performance, as well as individualized instructional and intervention needs.

> This column lists the instructional content for the week that is assessed in each item.

Question	Answer	Content Focus	CCSS	Complexity

> MSR item

> This column lists alignment for each assessment item.

> This column lists the Depth of Knowledge associated with each item.

Question	Answer	Content Focus	CCSS	Complexity
7	B, E	Main Idea and Key Details	RI.6.1, RI.6.2	DOK 3
8	D	Context Clues	RI.6.1, RI.6.4, L.6.4a	DOK 2
9A	C	Main Idea and Key Details	RI.6.1, RI.6.2	DOK 3
9B	B	Main Idea and Key Details	RI.6.1, RI.6.2	DOK 2

Comprehension: Selected Response 3, 4A, 4B, 8A, 8B, 9, 10A, 10B, 11A, 11B, 12A, 12B, 14	/16	%
Comprehension: Constructed Response 5, 15	/6	%
Vocabulary 1, 2A, 2B, 6A, 6B, 7, 13A, 13B	/10	%
English Language Conventions 16–25	/10	%
Total Unit Assessment Score	/42	%

> Scoring rows identify items by assessment focus and item type and allow for quick record keeping.

Performance-Based Assessments

The expectation is for students to score 80% or higher on the PBA:

- Narrative Writing: 20/25 on the entire task and 12/15 on the PCR
- Research Simulation: 30/37 on the entire task and 16/19 on the PCR
- Literary Analysis: 25/31 on the entire task and 16/19 on the PCR

This column lists alignment for each assessment item.

Unit 3 Assessment: Literary Analysis Task

Question	Answer	CCSS	Complexity
5A	A	RL.6.1, RL.6.2	DOK 3
5B	C		DOK 2
6	see below	RL.6.1, RL.6.3	DOK 2
7	see below	RL.6.1, RL.6.9 W.6.1, W.6.4-W.6.10 L.6.1, L.6.2, L.6.3, L.6.6	DOK 4

Comprehension 2A, 2B, 3A, 3B, 5A, 5B, 6A, 6B	/8	%
Vocabulary 1A, 1B, 4A, 4B	/4	%
Prose Constructed Response 7	/4 [RC] /12 [WE] /3 [LC]	%
Total Literary Analysis Score	/31	%

Scoring rows identify items by item type and allow for quick record keeping.

This cell specifies the points allocated by the scoring rubric to reading comprehension [RC], written expression [WE], and English language conventions [LC].

Read the story "Desert Holiday." Then answer questions 1 through 5.

Desert Holiday

1 On the first day of spring vacation, Grandpa and I headed east bright and early—that is, once we got out of the driveway. Just as the car was backing out, he slammed on the brakes and demanded, "Now, Manny, have you got your sunglasses?"

2 "Grandpa, I have them on!"

3 "Oh, so you do! Well, I'm just making sure because you don't want to get caught in Death Valley without sunglasses. You might go blind from the glare!"

4 No matter where I went with him, Grandpa always asked this question about sunglasses. I almost regretted coming along.

5 Though I had never considered visiting a desert, Grandpa had talked me into going camping with him the week before. He said Death Valley National Park was one of the most fascinating places on Earth. However, after agreeing to go, I started wondering why it's called Death Valley.

6 "I thought you'd never ask!" Grandpa said, leaning forward with that eager expression that always promised a monologue. "It's the lowest, driest, hottest place in North America. The temperature has gotten up to 134 degrees in the shade—and 201 degrees on the ground. Apart from reptiles and rodents and amphibians that burrow underground, not many creatures can survive that kind of blistering heat. It can be a mighty hostile environment." Passing me the map, he instructed me to read out some place names.

7 "Badwater, Coffin Peak, Deadman Pass, Dry Bone Canyon, Furnace Creek—"

8 "Of course, not all of the park is low land," he continued. "Telescope Peak is over 11,000 feet. But even at 282 feet below sea level, the valley won't be blazing hot in April. We might freeze our noses off at night and in the morning see carpets of wildflowers. There are more than 1,000 plant species in Death Valley, including 50 that grow nowhere else—it isn't like anyplace else you've ever been!"

9 Pausing for a moment, he added slyly, "It's a lot more fun than video games."

10 He just couldn't resist saying that, I thought to myself. But Grandpa was hard to argue with, and at least a trip to the desert sounded like something to brag about when we got home.

GO ON →

11 That first day, we drove into the late afternoon, until Grandpa pulled off the highway at a scenic overlook to point out the never-ending view of the desert. "In a while we'll be down there," he said. "From here you can see why Death Valley is an oven, where the sun bakes the earth. It's part of the Mojave Desert and the Great Basin, surrounded on all sides by mountain ranges. Do you see that long white area? That was once an inland sea. The water evaporated ages ago, leaving salt deposits like a crust on the land."

12 "You mean *that's* where we're going?" It looked unbelievably barren and colorless, like the last place on Earth anyone would choose to go.

13 Pondering briefly, Grandpa responded, "There are things you can't see from here. But if you don't feel like exploring the natural wonders of the park, we can always find an old ghost town to poke around."

14 I wasn't sure that sounded like a better option.

15 That night, Grandpa insisted on spreading our sleeping bags on the desert floor. Lying there, he explained why we could see so many more stars in Death Valley than we could in town. "There aren't any bright lights here, and the atmosphere is clear and dry, so you aren't looking through air that reflects light and hides the stars." Transfixed by the night's sky, he pointed out one constellation after another. As I drifted off to sleep, I repeated their names, over and over.

16 Over the next few days, we explored the desert, climbing huge sand dunes and wandering through canyons where the rock walls were so high and narrow the sky was barely visible. We hiked a mile and a half around the rim of Ubehebe Crater, part of an extinct volcano. At Racetrack Playa, we stared at heavy rocks that had mysteriously made tracks across the ground. "No one ever sees it happen," Grandpa said. "What could make them slide?"

17 On the final day, we saw a rainbow, got caught in a snow shower, and waited out a sandstorm in the car.

18 "Grandpa," I said as we were driving home, "that vacation was not what I expected." Among other wonders, I had seen colors in the desert land and sky, a sandstorm and a volcano, and too many constellations to count. I was even beginning to enjoy the stillness—not a single jet had roared overhead. Not once had I felt bored or even missed my games.

19 "Well, next time you can choose our destination," Grandpa said, clearly misunderstanding what I meant. "Where would you like to go?"

20 "The desert," I said, smiling. "Like, maybe Death Valley again."

GO ON →

1 **Part A**

Read the sentence from paragraph 6.

> "I thought you'd never ask!" Grandpa said, leaning forward with that eager expression that always promised a monologue.

The word **monologue** comes from two Greek roots, *mono-* and *log-*. *Log-* means "word" or "study." What does *mono-* mean?

(A) alone

(B) short

(C) two

(D) written

Part B

Based on the answer to Part A and details from the story, what is the definition of the word **monologue**?

(A) a short story in a book

(B) a long talk by a single speaker

(C) a conversation between two people

(D) a letter sent from one person to another

GO ON →

2 **Part A**

What does the word **hostile** mean as it is used in paragraph 6?

- (A) dry
- (B) lively
- (C) harsh
- (D) burning

Part B

Which **three** details from the story **best** support the answer to Part A?

- (A) "'. . . the lowest, driest, hottest place in North America . . .'" (paragraph 6)
- (B) "'. . . temperature has gotten up to 134 degrees in the shade . . .'" (paragraph 6)
- (C) "'. . . reptiles and rodents . . .'" (paragraph 6)
- (D) "'. . . amphibians that burrow underground . . .'" (paragraph 6)
- (E) "'. . . not many creatures can survive that kind of blistering heat.'" (paragraph 6)
- (F) "'. . . the valley won't be blazing hot in April . . .'" (paragraph 8)
- (G) "'. . . more than 1,000 plant species in Death Valley . . .'" (paragraph 8)

GO ON →

3 **Part A**

Why is Manny unsure about going to Death Valley at the beginning of the story?

- (A) He does not think it will be interesting.
- (B) He dislikes camping and being outdoors.
- (C) He will not be able to take his video games.
- (D) He is worried that the weather will be too hot.

Part B

Which detail from the story **best** supports the answer to Part A?

- (A) "But Grandpa was hard to argue with, and at least a trip to the desert sounded like something to brag about when we got home." (paragraph 10)
- (B) "That first day, we drove into the late afternoon, until Grandpa pulled off the highway at a scenic overlook to point out the never-ending view of the desert." (paragraph 11)
- (C) "It looked unbelievably barren and colorless, like the last place on Earth anyone would choose to go." (paragraph 12)
- (D) "We hiked a mile and a half around the rim of Ubehebe Crater, part of an extinct volcano." (paragraph 16)

GO ON →

4 Number each sentence 1, 2, 3, 4, 5, or 6 to show the correct sequence of the events in the story.

_____ Grandpa and Manny explore the desert for the next few days.

_____ Manny is surprised that he never felt bored or missed his video games.

_____ Manny feels unsure that camping with his Grandpa will be fun.

_____ Grandpa and Manny set up camp, and Grandpa shows Manny the constellations in the sky.

_____ Manny sees the view of Death Valley and is not impressed.

_____ Manny wonders why it is called "Death Valley."

GO ON →

5 **Part A**

How do Manny's feelings about the trip change over the course of the story?

Ⓐ At first, he is eager. After seeing the desert, he wishes he had stayed home.

Ⓑ At first, he is eager. When he finds out how long it will take, he is disappointed.

Ⓒ At first, he is not interested. After he sees and learns about the desert, he is enthusiastic.

Ⓓ At first, he does not want to go. When he gets in the car, he knows that he made the right choice.

Part B

Which detail from the story **best** supports the answer to Part A?

Ⓐ "No matter where I went with him, Grandpa always asked this question about sunglasses. I almost regretted coming along." (paragraph 4)

Ⓑ "That first day, we drove into the late afternoon, until Grandpa pulled off the highway at a scenic overlook to point out the never-ending view of the desert." (paragraph 11)

Ⓒ "Over the next few days, we explored the desert, climbing huge sand dunes and wandering through canyons where the rock walls were so high and narrow the sky was barely visible." (paragraph 16)

Ⓓ "'Grandpa,' I said as we were driving home, 'that vacation was not what I expected.' Among other wonders, I had seen colors in the desert land and sky, a sandstorm and a volcano, and too many constellations to count." (paragraph 18)

GO ON →

Read the article "The Mysterious Olm." Then answer questions 6 through 10.

The Mysterious Olm

1   How long could you survive in the subterranean world of a dark cave? Probably not 100 years—but then, that's only natural. After all, you aren't a troglobite! Troglobites are creatures that have adapted to life in caves. Some have adapted so well that they have lost features they don't need in darkness, such as sight and skin color. Many have developed other features that help them thrive in their underground habitat.

What's in a Name?

2   One rare creature has adapted especially well: a cave salamander called the "olm," whose scientific name is *Proteus anguinus.*

3   In Greek myths, Proteus was a god known as "the old man of the sea." He could tell anyone about the past, present, or future. However, he didn't always wish to share his knowledge. When Proteus preferred, he could suddenly vanish by changing his appearance, taking the form of a young man, a serpent, a fish, or something else. The Latin word *anguinus* means "snaky." It comes from the Latin word for "snake" or "dragon."

4   The scientific name of this salamander is appropriate. Centuries ago, people thought the olm resembled a baby dragon. These days, you might say it slithers like a snake and swims like a tadpole. But unlike a snake, the olm has legs; and unlike a tadpole, it does not change its shape.

Biology

5   All salamanders, as well as frogs and toads, are amphibians. Some breathe underwater through gills before developing lungs to breathe with on land. Like all amphibians, they are cold-blooded and have backbones. Their skin has a slimy coating rather than hair, feathers, or scales. They also absorb oxygen and other substances through their skin, which must be kept cool and moist. Most species breed by laying eggs in water.

6   The adult olm grows to a length of about 30 centimeters, or about 12 inches, and the female is somewhat larger than the male. The olm's body is long and slender with a flat tail. It has four small legs, three tiny toes on its front feet, and two tiny toes on its hind feet. Its head is wide and long with a rounded snout. On either side of its head are gills that stick out like tufts of feathers. The olm never loses its tail or its gills. However, as it matures, it also develops lungs.

GO ON →

7 Another feature sets the olm apart. Unlike most creatures (including its own cousins), the olm can live more than 100 years. Scientists have yet to discover why.

8 Like other cave salamanders, the olm survives on a diet of insects, snails, and crabs. But over 20 million years of living in dark caves, it has become mostly blind. It does have eyes that are almost microscopic, but they stop developing early in its life. Gradually, layers of skin grow over them. But the olm doesn't need its eyes to locate its prey. Instead, it relies on its super keen senses of smell and hearing.

9 The olm's skin is pale pink and translucent. Underneath, the shapes of its internal organs can be seen. Scientists think the olm's skin may also be a source of information, feeling tiny vibrations in the air and water that help the olm sense the presence of moving things.

Threats and Protection

10 Because of how they absorb substances through their skin, all amphibians are vulnerable to, or easily hurt by, air and water pollution. For millions of years, the olm has lived safely in subterranean caves in parts of central Europe. However, the water inside these caves has become increasingly polluted due to chemicals seeping down into it from cities and farmlands above. As a result, the olm's survival is threatened.

11 The olm is native to Croatia and Slovenia, where it even appears on a coin. Although the olm has become a tourist attraction in some countries, in parts of Europe the creature lives in special cave laboratories established to study and protect it. In one cave in France, a laboratory has been designed to resemble the olm's natural habitat. Since 1958, scientists there have been breeding and studying olms, yet they are still baffled by their unusually long lives. Through their studies, the scientists hope to ensure the survival of this rare and mysterious creature.

GO ON →

6 **Part A**

Read the sentence from paragraph 1.

> How long could you survive in the subterranean world of a dark cave?

The word **subterranean** contains the prefix *sub-*, which means "under," and the word *terranean,* which comes from the Greek root *terra*. What does the word *terra* **most likely** mean?

(A) cave

(B) darkness

(C) ground

(D) nature

Part B

Which sentence from paragraph 1 **best** supports the answer to Part A?

(A) "Probably not 100 years—but then, that's only natural."

(B) "Troglobites are creatures that have adapted to life in caves."

(C) "Some have adapted so well that they have lost features they don't need in darkness, such as sight and skin color."

(D) "Many have developed other features that help them thrive in their underground habitat."

GO ON →

7 **Part A**

Read the sentences from paragraph 9.

> The olm's skin is pale pink and translucent. Underneath, the shapes of its internal organs can be seen.

The word **translucent** comes from the prefix *trans-* and the Greek word *lucere*, which means "to shine." What does the prefix *trans-* **most likely** mean?

(A) around

(B) below

(C) inside

(D) through

Part B

Based on the answer to Part A and the details in the article, which definition **best** fits the meaning of the word **translucent**?

(A) to be lit up

(B) to glow from the inside

(C) able to be seen through

(D) looking like nearby objects

GO ON →

8 Which **two** features describe olms and which **two** features describe all cave salamanders? Draw lines from "olms" and "all cave salamanders" to **each** feature listed on the right.

Features

| olms |

| have a diet of insects, snails, and crabs |

| have translucent skin that shows their internal organs |

| all cave salamanders |

| have gills that look like tufts of feathers |

| can absorb oxygen and other substances through their skin |

GO ON →

Grade 6 • Unit Assessment • Unit 1

9 **Part A**

Which sentence **best** states a central idea of the article?

(A) The olm is mainly of interest to scientists.

(B) The olm has changed little in the past 20 million years.

(C) The olm has adapted especially well to its environment.

(D) The olm is one of the most cherished animals in Europe.

Part B

Which **two** details from the article **best** support the answer to Part A?

(A) "These days, you might say it slithers like a snake and swims like a tadpole. But unlike a snake, the olm has legs; and unlike a tadpole, it does not change its shape." (paragraph 4)

(B) "Like all amphibians, they are cold-blooded and have backbones. Their skin has a slimy coating rather than hair, feathers, or scales." (paragraph 5)

(C) "The adult olm grows to a length of about 30 centimeters, or about 12 inches, and the female is somewhat larger than the male. The olm's body is long and slender with a flat tail." (paragraph 6)

(D) "But the olm doesn't need its eyes to locate its prey. Instead, it relies on its super keen senses of smell and hearing." (paragraph 8)

(E) "Scientists think the olm's skin may also be a source of information. It may feel tiny vibrations in the air and water that help the olm sense the presence of moving things." (paragraph 9)

(F) "In one cave in France, a laboratory has been designed to resemble the olm's natural habitat." (paragraph 11)

GO ON →

10 What is the author's point of view regarding the olm? Support your
answer with details from the article.

_____

_____

_____

_____

_____

_____

_____

_____

Today you will read an article and a story about inventions.

Read the article "A Man with a Dream." Then answer questions 11 and 12.

A Man with a Dream

1   In the summer of 1821, inventor and mathematician Charles Babbage was checking the numbers in some tables and finding error after error. "I wish these calculations had been made by steam!" Babbage exclaimed. If only there were a steam machine that could make perfect calculations.

Invention

2   Soon, Babbage was designing a machine that could work mathematical problems in a logical way. He called it the Difference Engine. This machine was far ahead of its time, and Babbage had to make the tools needed to build its many parts. The Difference Engine interested scientist Sir Humphry Davy, who encouraged Babbage and persuaded the British government to pay some of the costs.

3   In the years that followed, Babbage found ways to improve his design. By 1830, his design called for 25,000 parts. Had all those parts been made and assembled, the machine would have stood 8 feet tall and weighed 15 tons! But the original Difference Engine was never completed. Babbage could be difficult to get along with, and he stopped work on it after having an argument with his engineer.

Improvement

4   In 1847, he began designing another model, Difference Engine No. 2. This new design called for 8,000 parts. It would weigh 5 tons and stand 8 feet tall.

5   Despite his years of work on them, Babbage never produced a finished computer. Government leaders became impatient and started rejecting his projects. They had given Babbage as much money as it would have cost to build 22 steam locomotives, and they still had nothing to show for it. So they withdrew their support. Babbage became discouraged and angry.

Frustration

6   Babbage's bitterness influenced his relationships with people. Once he became upset with the organ grinders who played in the street near his home, disturbing his train of thought. He began a long court battle to silence them. Instead, the organ grinders came from miles around to play beneath his windows.

GO ON →

7 Many people now doubted that the inventor's designs would even work. "Babbage Rhymes with Cabbage," a London newspaper headline announced in the 1860s. Babbage kept working on his computer, but he never completed it. He died an unhappy, disappointed person.

Success

8 Nearly 100 years later, in 1944, the world's first practical computer was finally built. A newspaper headline read, "Babbage's Dream Comes True."

9 In 2002, Difference Engine No. 2 was finally built in England. A team of experts had worked on the project for 17 years, making the parts and assembling them according to Babbage's design. By modern standards, the finished computer is a dinosaur. But its movements are wonderful to see, and it calculates and prints numbers perfectly.

GO ON →

11 **Part A**

What does the phrase "is a dinosaur" as it is used in paragraph 9 suggest about Babbage's computer?

(A) It is rare.   (C) It is outdated.

(B) It is powerful.   (D) It is dangerous.

Part B

Which detail from the article **best** supports the answer to Part A?

(A) "It would weigh 5 tons and stand 8 feet tall." (paragraph 4)

(B) "They had given Babbage as much money as it would have cost to build 22 new steam locomotives, and they still had nothing to show for it." (paragraph 5)

(C) "A team of experts had worked on the project for 17 years, making all the parts and putting them together according to Babbage's design." (paragraph 9)

(D) "But its movements are wonderful to see, and it calculates and prints numbers perfectly." (paragraph 9)

12 How does the author support the point of view that Babbage did not get along with people? Mark the box next to **two** details from the article that support the author's point of view.

Point of View: Babbage did not get along with people.

	His idea was inspired by errors someone had made in a table of numbers.
	He had to make the tools needed to build parts for the Difference Engine.
	After giving up on the Difference Engine, he started on a new project.
	Organ grinders traveled miles to play outside his home.
	The government gave him a lot of money but had no product to show for it.
	A newspaper published an article titled "Babbage Rhymes with Cabbage."

GO ON →

Read the story "A Light for Learning." Then answer questions 13 and 14.

A Light for Learning

1   Each day after school, Amani helped his father tend the yam fields and repair farm equipment. By the time they returned home for dinner, the village was dark and there was not enough light for Amani to finish his homework. Electricity had not yet reached this remote village, and his family owned only two oil lamps that they used sparingly because oil was so expensive.

2   This day was different, though, as Amani's teacher Mr. Nicoi had presented each student with a special soccer ball. Inside each ball was a mini generator that harnessed the energy of the ball's movement, generating useable power. The more the ball was moved, the more energy it created, and each ball came with a small lamp that plugged into a socket on the ball. "Playing with this ball for thirty minutes will generate three hours of power for the lamps," he told the class.

3   The sun was setting as Amani and his father headed home from the yam fields. They dribbled the soccer ball on the long walk. When Amani plugged in the lamp, a strong beam of light shone out. The generator really worked! After dinner, Amani found his math homework and worked to solve the problems. Then he read a book from the library about how machines and inventions operated. He was intrigued by how things worked, devouring any information he could find. He brought the book to bed, along with the lamp. It was the first night ever that Amani had the luxury of reading in bed. "Go to sleep, Amani," his mother called to him an hour later.

4   The next morning, when Amani proudly turned in his homework, he felt the world open its doors to him. He thought of all he could achieve with three more hours of light each night. That evening, Amani kicked the soccer ball back from the fields as hard as he could, hoping to generate the maximum amount of energy.

5   After dinner, he plugged in the lamp to the ball, but the lamp didn't turn on. Amani checked the light bulb and the power cord. When he shook the ball, he heard a clanking sound. Heartbroken, he realized he damaged the generator inside the ball by kicking it too hard.

6   Amani knew his school couldn't afford a replacement. Now he would never finish his homework and never learn all the things he imagined he could. The world would close its doors to him again. He resolved to wake up at first light and repair the generator.

GO ON →

7 At dawn, Amani hunted through the shed for tools. He pried open the ball and cut through a layer of rubber to peer into the heart of the generator. Inside was a battery and wires connected to a mechanism with a gear. Amani saw a piece of unattached plastic. He reattached the piece of plastic and sealed up the ball again with glue. He waited for it to dry and worried about Mr. Nicoi's reaction.

8 Amani was afraid to kick the ball, so he shook it with his hands the entire way to school. When the light turned on, Mr. Nicoi claimed he wasn't surprised at all. "You clearly have an eye for how things work." His classmate Grace showed Amani that her ball had broken, too. Amani promised to take a look at it that night, using the light of his own generator. After all, everyone deserved a light for learning.

GO ON →

13 **Part A**

What is the main problem at the beginning of the story?

(A) Amani cannot complete his homework.

(B) Amani has too many chores after school.

(C) The generator in the soccer ball is too weak.

(D) There is not enough time to play with the soccer ball.

Part B

Which sentence from the story **best** supports the answer to Part A?

(A) "Each day after school, Amani helped his father tend the yam fields and repair farm equipment." (paragraph 1)

(B) "By the time they returned home for dinner, the village was dark and there was not enough light for Amani to finish his homework." (paragraph 1)

(C) "Inside each ball was a mini generator that harnessed the energy of the ball's movement, generating useable power." (paragraph 2)

(D) "'Playing with this ball for thirty minutes will generate three hours of power for the lamps,' he told the class." (paragraph 2)

14 Read the sentences from paragraph 8 of the story.

When the light turned on, Mr. Nicoi claimed he wasn't surprised at all. "You clearly have an eye for how things work."

Which paragraph from the story **best** supports Mr. Nicoi's statement?

(A) paragraph 4

(B) paragraph 5

(C) paragraph 6

(D) paragraph 7

GO ON →

Name: _____ Date: _____

Refer to the article "A Man with a Dream" and the story "A Light for Learning." Then answer question 15.

15 The article "A Man with a Dream" and the story "A Light for Learning" describe ideas with great potential for changing the way people look at the world. These new ideas come with new challenges. Explain the different ways Charles Babbage and Amani react to these challenges. Use details from the texts to support your answer.

_____

_____

_____

_____

_____

_____

_____

_____

_____

_____

_____

_____

GO ON →

Name: _____ Date: _____

The following passage needs revision. Read the passage. Then answer questions 16 through 25.

(1) Last summer, Jason tried snorkeling, he did it for the first time. (2) He was visiting his friend Jeremy in Hawaii during the vacation. (3) What a great place.

(4) Secretly, Jason hated swimming. (5) But Jeremy said he should try this or go back home.

(6) "Why do I have to learn snorkeling" Jason.

(7) "You have to try snorkeling when you're in Hawaii. (8) If not snorkeling, then you have to try surfing."

(9) So Jason and Jeremy floated off beyond the waves. (10) Jeremy swam like a fish. (11) Jason tried to follow. (12) He could not keep up. (13) He and Jeremy were not swimming the same way. (14) Because it wasn't fastened on right, Jason had lost one of his fins. (15) He kicked off the other one, that made all the difference.

(16) Finally, things got easier. (17) Jason looked down into the water and realized why they were out there in the first place. (18) He saw the fish and the plants and the coral reef below them. (19) The sea was full of life and colors. (20) He could hardly wait to tell his friends about this. (21) He got home.

16 How can sentence 1 **best** be written?

(A) Last summer Jason snorkeled and he did it for the first time.

(B) Last summer, Jason tried snorkeling for the first time.

(C) For the first time last summer, Jason tried, snorkeling.

(D) Snorkeling, Jason tried last summer, for the first time.

17 Which sentence needs an exclamation mark because it is exclamatory?

(A) Sentence 2

(B) Sentence 3

(C) Sentence 4

(D) Sentence 5

18 What is the **best** way to write sentence 6?

(A) "Why do I have to learn snorkeling, Jason."

(B) "Why do I have to learn snorkeling," Jason.

(C) "Why do I have to learn snorkeling!" Jason asked.

(D) "Why do I have to learn snorkeling?" Jason asked.

19 How can sentences 7 and 8 **best** be combined?

(A) "You either have to try snorkeling or surfing when you're in Hawaii."

(B) "You have to try snorkeling in Hawaii, or you have to try surfing in Hawaii."

(C) "You have to try snorkeling when you're in Hawaii, you have to try surfing."

(D) "When you're in Hawaii, you have to try snorkeling, you have to try surfing."

GO ON →

20 What is the complete subject of sentence 9?

(A) Jason and Jeremy

(B) Jason and Jeremy floated

(C) beyond the waves

(D) floated beyond the waves

21 Which is the **best** way to combine sentences 11 and 12 to make a compound sentence?

(A) Jason tried to follow, he could not keep up.

(B) Jason tried to follow, but he could not keep up.

(C) Jason tried to follow he could not keep up.

(D) Jason tried to follow, so he could not keep up.

22 Which sentence contains a dependent clause?

(A) Sentence 9

(B) Sentence 10

(C) Sentence 13

(D) Sentence 14

23 Which is a run-on sentence?

(A) Sentence 13

(B) Sentence 15

(C) Sentence 16

(D) Sentence 17

GO ON →

24 What is the complete predicate of sentence 19?

    Ⓐ The sea

    Ⓑ The sea was

    Ⓒ full of life and colors

    Ⓓ was full of life and colors

25 Which is the **best** way to combine sentences 20 and 21?

    Ⓐ He could hardly wait to tell his friends about this when he got home.

    Ⓑ He could hardly wait to tell his friends about this, and he got home.

    Ⓒ He could hardly wait to tell his friends about this, or he got home.

    Ⓓ He could hardly wait to tell his friends about this so he got home.

STOP

Narrative Writing Task

Today you will read "Sniffles," a mystery story. As you read and answer the questions, pay close attention to the plot and characters to help prepare you to write a narrative story.

Read the story "Sniffles." Then answer questions 1 through 6.

Sniffles

1   I pulled the blankets up to my chin, hoping I could stay in bed for five more minutes. Then I remembered that it was Saturday and suddenly felt wide awake. I was still freezing, though, so before I went down to breakfast, I looked for my robe. There it was, balled up on the closet floor right next to my backpack.

2   I'd dumped my pack in there yesterday when I got home from Julia's house, where four of us had met to pick a History topic and assign tasks for our group project. Groaning, I remembered all the work I had to finish before Monday. Resolving not to open my backpack until tomorrow, I shrugged into my bathrobe and went downstairs.

3   "Good morning, Hal—breakfast is almost ready!" Dad waved his spatula at me and turned back to the stove, where something was sizzling on the grill.

4   "It's pancakes," said my sister Amy, who had just turned five. "Can I have the first one, Hal?"

5   "Sure," I shrugged, sitting down as Mom wandered into the kitchen holding the phone.

6   "Hal—it's Julia's mother," she said, "wondering whether you saw their kitten when you were over there yesterday—apparently, Sniffles is missing."

7   "Nope—Julia's mom usually puts him upstairs when people come over because he just crawls on everyone's homework papers and meows until you pet him . . . plus, I'm allergic."

8   Mom left to hang up the phone, then joined Dad at the stove, and soon, they brought a steaming plate of pancakes to the table. Spearing the top pancake with my fork, I plopped it on Amy's plate, but she just stared at it, frowning.

9   "What's the matter? I thought you wanted the first one," I said.

10   "What's going to happen to Sniffles, Mommy?" Amy asked.

GO ON →

11 "Oh, he probably crawled into a cozy little corner for a nice, long nap—don't worry."

12 Amy looked doubtful, but the smell of Dad's pancakes was enough to distract anyone. Meanwhile, I grabbed a pancake, admiring it as it dangled from my fork, a perfect golden-brown. Suddenly, I felt a tickling sensation in my nostrils.

13 "Ah-CHOO!" I sneezed with a violent jerking motion that sent my pancake flying across the table.

14 "Good thing I made extra," said Dad, tossing the pancake in the garbage and serving me another.

15 Feeling another sneeze coming on, I pushed back from the table, grabbed a box of tissues, turned my face away, and sneezed five, six times. When I returned to the table, everyone was staring at me.

16 "Are you coming down with a cold?" Mom asked.

17 "No, I feel fine," I said, pouring syrup on my pancake.

18 "Why are your eyes all red?" Amy asked.

19 I shrugged, but come to think of it, they *were* feeling kind of itchy, so I rubbed them, which only made it worse. Then I grabbed a tissue and sneezed again.

20 "Maybe it's allergies," I said, "except it's November, and they usually only bother me in the spring."

21 "Sniffles wouldn't happen to be orange and white, would he?" Dad pointed to my blue terrycloth bathrobe, which had somehow sprouted patches of orange and white hair. "Perhaps Sniffles is causing your sniffles."

22 "That's impossible," I said, jumping up from my chair and running upstairs as my family followed behind. "He must have crawled into my backpack at Julia's, and slept last night on my robe."

23 I opened the closet and flicked on the light to find Sniffles, curled up on the floor on top of a T-shirt. I *had* to start hanging up my clothes.

GO ON →

1 **Part A**

How does paragraph 6 help develop the plot of the story?

(A) It leads to the climax.

(B) It introduces the conflict.

(C) It increases the suspense level.

(D) It signals a decrease in the action.

Part B

Which detail from the story **best** supports the answer to Part A?

(A) "I pulled the blankets up to my chin, hoping I could stay in bed for five more minutes." (paragraph 1)

(B) "Groaning, I remembered all the work I had to finish before Monday." (paragraph 2)

(C) "'It's pancakes,' said my sister Amy, who had just turned five. 'Can I have the first one, Hal?'" (paragraph 4)

(D) "'What's going to happen to Sniffles, Mommy?' Amy asked." (paragraph 10)

GO ON →

2 **Part A**

Which statement **best** describes how paragraphs 1 and 2 fit into the overall structure of the story?

(A) They provide clues to solving the mystery.

(B) They indicate a change in Hal's character.

(C) They state Hal's major problem.

(D) They represent a flashback.

Part B

Which detail from the story plays the same role as the answer to Part A?

(A) "Dad waved his spatula at me and turned back to the stove, where something was sizzling on the grill." (paragraph 3)

(B) "'. . . he just crawls on everyone's homework papers and meows until you pet him . . . plus, I'm allergic.'" (paragraph 7)

(C) "Spearing the top pancake with my fork, I plopped it on Amy's plate, but she just stared at it, frowning." (paragraph 8)

(D) "'Good thing I made extra,' said Dad, tossing the pancake in the garbage and serving me another." (paragraph 14)

GO ON →

3 **Part A**

Which statement **best** describes Amy's response to the news about Sniffles's disappearance?

(A) She is concerned, but not so much that she loses her appetite.

(B) She is extremely worried because she has a special attachment to the cat.

(C) She is not overly concerned, figuring that the cat will turn up soon.

(D) She is intrigued and makes it her responsibility to solve the mystery.

Part B

Which detail from the story **best** supports the answer to Part A?

(A) "'It's pancakes,' said my sister Amy, who had just turned five. 'Can I have the first one, Hal?'" (paragraph 4)

(B) "Spearing the top pancake with my fork, I plopped it on Amy's plate, but she just stared at it, frowning." (paragraph 8)

(C) "Amy looked doubtful, but the smell of Dad's pancakes was enough to distract anyone." (paragraph 12)

(D) "When I returned to the table, everyone was staring at me." (paragraph 15)

GO ON →

4 **Part A**

Which sentence **best** describes how the characters contribute to the resolution in the story?

(A) Hal has a sneezing fit and connects this clue to Sniffles's disappearance.

(B) Dad notices the cat hair and Hal uses this clue to figure out what happened to Sniffles.

(C) Amy points out Hal's allergy symptoms and Dad uses this clue to discover the cat hair.

(D) Mom asks Hal whether he has a cold and Hal uses this clue to realize he is having an allergy attack.

Part B

Which **two** details from the story, when taken together, **best** support the answer to Part A?

(A) "Feeling another sneeze coming on, I pushed back from the table, grabbed a box of tissues, turned my face away, and sneezed five, six times." (paragraph 15)

(B) "'Are you coming down with a cold?' Mom asked." (paragraph 16)

(C) "'Why are your eyes all red?' Amy asked." (paragraph 18)

(D) "'Maybe it's allergies,' I said, 'except it's November, and they usually only bother me in the spring.'" (paragraph 20)

(E) "'Sniffles wouldn't happen to be orange and white, would he?'" (paragraph 21)

(F) "'He must have crawled into my backpack at Julia's, and slept last night on my robe.'" (paragraph 22)

GO ON →

5 Which details from the story would be important to include in a summary? Write four details in the chart in chronological order.

	Details
1	
2	
3	
4	

Details

Hal hopes to stay in bed an extra five minutes.
Dad decides to make pancakes for breakfast.
Hal discovers Sniffles sleeping next to his backpack.
Amy worries about what will happen to Sniffles.
Hal suddenly starts having an allergy attack.
Dad notices cat hair on Hal's robe.
Hal decides to take Saturday off.
Julia's mom calls to say that Sniffles is missing.

6 In the story "Sniffles," the author develops a mystery that centers on a character named Hal. Think about the details the author uses to establish the mystery and create the main character. The story begins with Hal reflecting on a project meeting he attended the day before.

Write an original story about what happens at that meeting—including how Sniffles manages to stow away in Hal's backpack. In your "prequel," be sure to use what you have learned about Hal as you describe what happens before "Sniffles" begins.

Write your story on a separate sheet of paper.

STOP

Answer Key

Name: _____

Question	Correct Answer	Content Focus	CCSS	Complexity
1A	A	Greek Roots	RL.6.1, RL.6.4, L.6.4b	DOK 1
1B	B	Greek Roots	RL.6.1, RL.6.4, L.6.4b	DOK 1
2A	C	Context Clues: Paragraph Clues	RL.6.1, RL.6.4, L.6.4a	DOK 2
2B	A, B, E	Context Clues: Paragraph Clues	RL.6.1, RL.6.4, L.6.4a	DOK 2
3A	A	Character, Setting, Plot: Sequence	RL.6.1, RL.6.3	DOK 2
3B	C	Character, Setting, Plot: Sequence	RL.6.1, RL.6.3	DOK 2
4	see below	Character, Setting, Plot: Sequence	RL.6.1, RL.6.3	DOK 2
5A	C	Character, Setting, Plot: Compare and Contrast	RL.6.1, RL.6.3	DOK 2
5B	D	Character, Setting, Plot: Compare and Contrast	RL.6.1, RL.6.3	DOK 2
6A	C	Greek Roots	RI.6.1, RI.6.4, L.6.4b	DOK 1
6B	D	Greek Roots	RI.6.1, RI.6.4, L.6.4b	DOK 1
7A	D	Greek Roots	RI.6.1, RI.6.4, L.6.4b	DOK 1
7B	C	Greek Roots	RI.6.1, RI.6.4, L.6.4b	DOK 1
8	see below	Main Idea and Key Details	RI.6.1, RI.6.2	DOK 2
9A	C	Main Idea and Key Details	RI.6.1, RI.6.2	DOK 2
9B	D, E	Main Idea and Key Details	RI.6.1, RI.6.2	DOK 2
10	see below	Author's Point of View	RI.6.1, RI.6.6	DOK 3
11A	C	Metaphors and Similes	RI.6.1, RI.6.4, L.6.5a	DOK 2
11B	A	Metaphors and Similes	RI.6.1, RI.6.4, L.6.5a	DOK 2
12	see below	Author's Point of View	RI.6.1, RI.6.6	DOK 3
13A	A	Character, Setting, Plot: Sequence	RL.6.1, RL.6.3	DOK 2
13B	B	Character, Setting, Plot: Sequence	RL.6.1, RL.6.3	DOK 2
14	D	Character, Setting, Plot: Sequence	RL.6.1, RL.6.3	DOK 3
15	see below	Compare Across Texts	W.6.9	DOK 4
16	B	Run-on Sentences and Comma Splices	L.6.2	DOK 1

Name: _____

Question	Correct Answer	Content Focus	CCSS	Complexity
17	B	Sentence Types and Fragments	L.6.2	DOK 1
18	D	Sentence Types and Fragments	L.6.2	DOK 1
19	A	Sentence Combining	L.6.2	DOK 1
20	A	Subjects and Predicates	L.6.1	DOK 1
21	B	Sentence Combining	L.6.2	DOK 1
22	D	Clauses and Complex Sentences	L.6.1	DOK 1
23	B	Run-on Sentences and Comma Splices	L.6.2	DOK 1
24	D	Subjects and Predicates	L.6.1	DOK 1
25	A	Clauses and Complex Sentences	L.6.1	DOK 1

Comprehension: Selected Response 3A, 3B, 4, 5A, 5B, 8, 9A, 9B, 12, 13A, 13B, 14	/16	%
Comprehension: Constructed Response 10, 15	/6	%
Vocabulary 1A, 1B, 2A, 2B, 6A, 6B, 7A, 7B, 11A, 11B	/10	%
English Language Conventions 16-25	/10	%
Total Unit Assessment Score	/42	%

4 Students should write the following numbers: 5, 6, 1, 4, 3, 2.

8 Students should match the following features:
- olms: have translucent skin that shows their internal organs; have gills that look like tufts of feathers
- all cave salamanders: can absorb oxygen and other substances through their skin; have a diet of insects, snakes, and crabs

10 **2-point response:** The author is clearly fascinated by the lifespan of the olm. He starts off the article by asking the reader how long they could survive in a cave and says "probably not 100 years." He then goes on to explain that olms live for 100 years and scientists cannot figure out why. He makes it sound interesting and mysterious and it shows his fascination with the subject. He even ends the article by saying olms are a "fascinating creature."

12 Students should mark the boxes next to the following details:
- Organ grinders traveled miles to play outside his home.
- A newspaper published an article titled "Babbage Rhymes with Cabbage."

15 **4-point response:** Charles Babbage in "A Man with a Dream" and Amani in "A Light for Learning" reacted in very different ways to new challenges. Amani had a love of learning, so he was very excited when the light-generating soccer ball gave him an opportunity to spend more time reading and studying. He understood how life-changing this invention was. When the ball was damaged shortly after he received it, he didn't become discouraged. Instead, he remained positive and "resolved to wake up at first light and repair the generator." He was unstoppable and successful. He was determined to overcome any obstacle to continue his education.

In contrast, Charles Babbage became easily frustrated and was not easy to work with. His first attempt at creating a successful steam computer failed because of an argument he had with his engineer. Later, when the government withdrew support because of all his delays, he became very "discouraged and angry." As a result, his major projects failed, he became the object of ridicule, and he "died an unhappy, disappointed person."

Answer Key

Name: _____

Unit 1 Assessment: Narrative Writing Task

Question	Answer	CCSS	Complexity
1A	B	RL.6.1, RL.6.3	DOK 2
1B	D		DOK 2
2A	A	RL.6.1, RL.6.5	DOK 2
2B	B		DOK 2
3A	A	RL.6.1, RL.6.3	DOK 2
3B	C		DOK 2
4A	B	RL.6.1, RL.6.3	DOK 3
4B	E, F		DOK 2
5	see below	RL.6.1, RL.6.2	DOK 2
6	see below	W.6.3–W.6.10 L.6.1, L.6.2, L.6.3, L.6.6	DOK 4

Comprehension 1A, 1B, 2A, 2B, 3A, 3B, 4A, 4B, 5	/10	%
Prose Constructed Response 6	/12 [WE] /3 [LC]	%
Total Narrative Writing Score	/25	%

5 Students should complete the chart as follows: 1—Julia's mom calls to say that Sniffles is missing.; 2—Hal suddenly starts having an allergy attack.; 3—Dad notices cat hair on Hal's robe.; 4—Hal discovers Sniffles sleeping next to his backpack.

6 15-point anchor paper:

The meeting had only started fifteen minutes ago, and already, I couldn't wait for it to end. We had decided to meet at Julia's house, which was just down the street from me. Julia, me, Marcus, and Rachel had been assigned to work together on a History project. Between soccer practice, choir rehearsals, and guitar lessons, we weren't all free until Friday after school—not the best time to focus on school, if you ask me.

I sat at Julia's kitchen table and opened my backpack with a groan. "Let's make this short and sweet," I said. I took out my History notebook and grabbed a pen before shoving my pack under the table.

"I'm all for short meetings," said Rachel, "as long as we make some progress. I mean, we've got a lot to do."

I like Rachel, but she tends to worry too much about every detail. I glanced at her notebook page, where she'd already written the date, time, and the heading, "History Project." In the margin, she'd listed the numbers 1 through 10, each one waiting to be filled in. And I hadn't even opened my notebook yet.

"I'm not sure about *short*, Hal," said Julia, "but I can do something about the *sweet*." She set a plate of cookies and fruit on the table.

We wasted about ten minutes snacking and stalling. Then Marcus cleared his throat and said, "Well?"

Whenever Marcus says something, people listen. He's smart and he understands how to solve problems. So I was glad he stepped in to give us some direction.

"Why don't we start by settling on a topic, then decide how we want to present it?" Marcus continued.

After a long silence, everyone jumped in, and we argued for a while about whether "Queens of the Nile" would be more interesting than "Egyptian Mummies." Then Julia's orange-and-white kitten jumped onto the table. Sniffles wandered around before settling on top of Julia's notebook to take a bath. Rachel and Marcus fussed over him and Sniffles licked every spot they'd just petted. Me—I just leaned away. Sniffles is really cute, but if he came too close, I'd probably start sneezing.

"Mom?" Julia called out. "Sniffles is interrupting our meeting!"

Julia's mom came to get Sniffles and we got back to planning. Our project idea was really cool, but the longer we met, the more involved it became. Just thinking about it was making me tired. I felt something furry brush my leg and looked down to see Sniffles was back. At least he stayed under the table where he couldn't bother anyone.

When we finished dividing up tasks, it felt like the weekend had finally arrived. I dragged out my backpack, slipped in my notebook, and zipped it up—well, it wouldn't zip back up all the way, but I didn't care. It was only one short block home. When I got there, I dumped my backpack in my closet, where I planned to leave it until Sunday.

Read the article "Going to America." Then answer questions 1 through 5.

Going to America

1   A young passenger named Jonas kept his balance and managed to stay upright on the deck of the ship. But it was a challenge as the wind screamed and howled and tried to throw him into the water. From below the deck came the moans and cries of seasick Pilgrims, who had been on the ship for weeks already and could not last much longer. The captain of the Mayflower maneuvered the ship through huge swells in the Atlantic Ocean on his way to America. He knew he was close to land because he could feel it in his bones; their journey was almost over. However, the captain did not realize that his ship was about 600 miles off course. The Pilgrims would not be landing where they had planned.

2   The people going to America were not called Pilgrims when they were living in England in the early 1600s. They were Puritans who became supporters of Separatism. They wanted to separate from the Church of England because they did not feel free to follow their own religious beliefs.

3   In 1608, a group of these Separatists left England and relocated to the city of Amsterdam in Holland. A year later, they moved again to the Dutch city of Leiden. Though they found some religious freedom there and stayed for a number of years, they were not allowed to govern themselves. They had to obey the rules and laws of Holland. Also, they could not earn enough money to support themselves. In 1617, members of the group decided to move to America. At that time, there were several small settlements in Virginia and in the New York area. The Leiden group got permission from the London Company, which controlled those colonies, to settle on part of their land.

4   That year, about half of the people in the Leiden group boarded a ship called the *Speedwell* and sailed back to England, where they joined up with another group of Separatists. They added a second ship, the *Mayflower*, to take them all to America. The *Speedwell* was a 60-ton ship, which is rather small for such a long voyage. The *Mayflower* was three times the size of the *Speedwell* and only about 12 years old. It had already proved itself on long voyages as a trading ship.

5   When all was ready, the group set sail from Plymouth, England, bound for the New World. Unfortunately, the *Speedwell* soon began to leak. Both ships returned to the harbor in England for repairs. When the ships departed a second time, the *Speedwell* again leaked. A full month later, the entire group of 102 passengers crowded onto the *Mayflower* and set sail once again.

GO ON →

6 Through many North Atlantic storms and 65 days at sea, the passengers on the *Mayflower* survived, finally reaching land near present-day Provincetown at the end of Cape Cod, Massachusetts. It was late November, and winter was approaching. They had permission to settle near Virginia, but that is not where they had landed. So they steered south for another day, hoping they could make it at least as far as New York. But the weather and the rocky shores were too dangerous, so they turned back and landed at Provincetown.

7 Soon after their arrival, these Separatists created a document called the Mayflower Compact. This was an agreement among the men on the ship as to how they would live and govern themselves. Led by a man named William Bradford, 41 men on the *Mayflower* signed this paper. All agreed to follow the rules of the group. Bradford was the first person to refer to these people as Pilgrims. With this document, the Pilgrims also agreed to settle in Massachusetts instead of in Virginia as they had planned.

8 Over the next few weeks, the Pilgrims searched for a good place to live. In late December, they found a harbor on the other end of Cape Cod at a place they called Plymouth. That is where they made their home that first winter, but they faced a number of obstacles. They had no shelter from the weather, and winter had already begun. They had very little food and could not plant any crops in December. By the following spring, about half of the colonists had died. In April of 1621 the *Mayflower* returned to England.

The Pilgrims' Voyage (1620–1621)

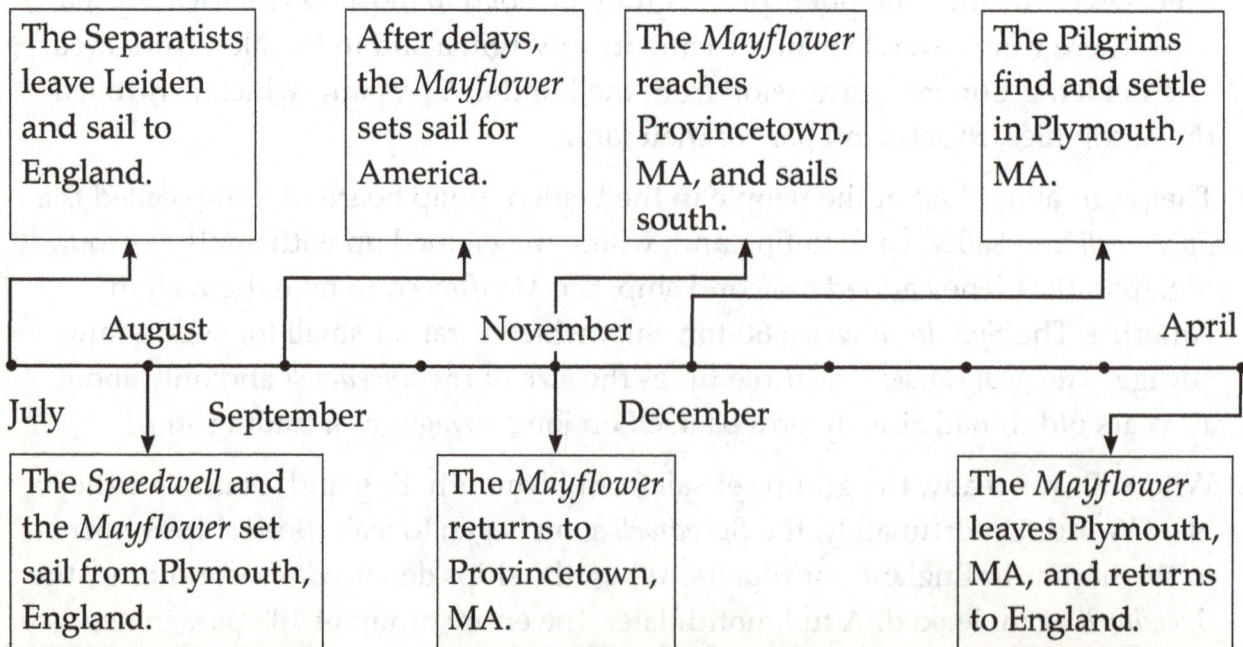

| The Separatists leave Leiden and sail to England. | After delays, the *Mayflower* sets sail for America. | The *Mayflower* reaches Provincetown, MA, and sails south. | The Pilgrims find and settle in Plymouth, MA. |

August   November   April

July   September   December

| The *Speedwell* and the *Mayflower* set sail from Plymouth, England. | The *Mayflower* returns to Provincetown, MA. | The *Mayflower* leaves Plymouth, MA, and returns to England. |

GO ON →

1 Part A

Read the sentence from paragraph 1 of the article.

> But it was a challenge as the wind screamed and howled and tried to throw him into the water.

Which statement **best** describes the effect of the personification used in the sentence?

(A) It helps show the apprehension the Pilgrims experienced.

(B) It shows how far away from land the Pilgrims were.

(C) It illustrates how exhausting and dangerous the journey was.

(D) It suggests that the captain was not experienced enough to lead the ship.

Part B

Which detail from paragraph 1 **best** supports the answer to Part A?

(A) "From below the deck came the moans and cries of seasick Pilgrims . . ."

(B) "He knew he was close to land because he could feel it in his bones . . ."

(C) "However, the captain did not realize that his ship was about 600 miles off course."

(D) "The Pilgrims would not be landing where they had planned."

GO ON →

2 **Part A**

Read the sentence from paragraph 3.

> In 1608, a group of these Separatists left England and relocated to the city of Amsterdam in Holland.

What does the word **relocated** suggest about what the Separatists did in Amsterdam?

(A) They visited Amsterdam again.

(B) They found Amsterdam on a map.

(C) They made a new home for themselves in Amsterdam.

(D) They created connections with people in Amsterdam.

Part B

Which **two** details from the article **best** help the reader determine the meaning of the word **relocated**?

(A) "... wanted to separate ..." (paragraph 2)

(B) "... did not feel free ..." (paragraph 2)

(C) "... moved again ..." (paragraph 3)

(D) "... had to obey the rules and laws ..." (paragraph 3)

(E) "... earn enough money to support themselves." (paragraph 3)

(F) "... got permission ... to settle ..." (paragraph 3)

GO ON →

3 Part A

How does paragraph 1 contribute to the development of ideas in the article?

(A) It shows how skilled the captain of the *Mayflower* was.

(B) It gives details about the *Mayflower*'s size and appearance.

(C) It describes the type of people that chose to set sail on the *Mayflower*.

(D) It provides a description of what the Pilgrims experienced on the *Mayflower*.

Part B

Which detail from the article **best** supports the answer to Part A?

(A) Many passengers were seasick below the deck.

(B) The ship had to battle against huge swells of water.

(C) The captain could feel when the ship was approaching land.

(D) Passengers on the deck sometimes had to be careful to hold on.

GO ON →

4 The author presents the idea that the Pilgrims were determined to succeed. First, write in the chart **one** main strategy used throughout the article to convey this idea. Then, write **two** details that best demonstrate the strategy.

Strategy	Details

Strategies:
by describing the Pilgrims' daily lives
by comparing the Pilgrims to previous settlers
by showing how the Pilgrims overcame problems
by explaining the Pilgrims' reasons for leaving Europe

Details:
The remaining Pilgrims returned to England after winter passed.

The entire group squeezed onto one ship and spent 65 days at sea.

The group set sail from England a month after they originally planned.

The men signed an agreement about the laws they would live by in America.

The Pilgrims attempted to live in Plymouth despite bad weather and lack of food.

GO ON →

Name: _____ Date: _____

5 Using information found in the article and the timeline, write a number from 1–6 next to each event to show the order in which they occurred.

_____ The group received permission to settle in Virginia.

_____ The group wanted to leave the Church of England.

_____ The *Mayflower* returned to England with the *Speedwell*.

_____ The group found Plymouth, MA.

_____ The Mayflower Compact was written and signed.

_____ The group became known as Pilgrims.

Read the story "My Adventures Through Time." Then answer questions 6 through 10.

My Adventures Through Time

1 I was recently vacationing in a desert near Arizona. I stretched my long body over a warm rock to enjoy the heat from the sun. Just as I was about to nap, a fellow reptile scuttled by and extended himself across the rock near mine. We exchanged polite "hellos" but before long, began to swap stories of our travels. I went on for what must have been hours, for the sun moved across the sky and disappeared beneath the horizon while I was yet still describing my early years. Wide-eyed, the young comrade asked me my age. I responded with a chuckle and told him that the year I hatched, the calendar to which he referred had not yet been invented. I told the lizard of a meal of exotic berries that I had eaten, and of the strange, long sleep that ensued. I slept for thousands of years—yet when I awoke it seemed as if I'd not aged a day. The berries had somehow made me immune to the effects of time.

2 "Were you scared?" the young lizard asked, his tiny jaw nearly hitting the ground.

3 "At first, but I decided that an adventure through time was an adventure worth taking, so I set out to explore the new world into which I'd awoken."

4 The young lizard begged me to tell him more of my adventures, and so I did.

. . .

5 In my early years, time as I knew it fell into two categories: day or night. Every morning the sun would ascend high into the sky and every night it would disappear beneath the earth.

6 "There were no clocks?" the young lizard asked.

7 I told him that my first memory of a time device was of a great sundial, built by the Egyptians. It divided the day into six segments and relied upon a shadow to reveal the time. Though I quite liked the way it looked, I was not a fan of precise methods to track time. Why did it matter if it was segment two or three of daylight? As long as I ate and slept, I was one content lizard.

8 The little lizard implored me to continue, and so I told him of how the Romans captured sundials from the Samnites and of how the Greeks built upon those inventions with their knowledge of geometry. Segments of time continued to be

GO ON →

refined until Apollonius of Perga further developed the accuracy of the sundial by adding lines representative of hours. Eventually, engineers began to create smaller, portable sundials.

9 "But when did the sundial become a clock?" the young lizard asked impatiently.

10 I explained that the first time I noticed what I would call an actual "clock" had to have been around 1300 AD when I was traveling across Europe. I happened upon a beautiful monastery in England and found a rock with a splash of sunlight, perfect for an afternoon nap. I was startled when a loud gong blasted through the air; I quite almost lost my tail!

11 I scurried inside the tower to search out the source of the loud noise and found a large, iron-framed structure with weights that were connected to a massive object. I interviewed some of the local wildlife to learn all I could about the strange structure that bellowed every hour. It was odd to me how the humans made plans to meet and disassemble based on the number of gongs.

12 I thought the mechanical clock would be the pinnacle of timepieces—until I met Galileo. He added a feature I quite liked: a great pendulum swung back and forth to mark time. For a lizard like me, it was a fun form of entertainment. Oh how high the pendulum would swing! It was an exhilarating ride.

13 But alas, time went by and people once again began to prefer smaller clocks and watches. The little gadgets did not afford me an entertaining ride. I had to wait until the train came along in the 1800s.

14 Oh, how I loved the feeling of the wind blowing through my scales. The train riders were very particular about schedules. They wanted to know exactly when a train would arrive and depart. Train time became the anchor to which all the citizens in a city would set their clocks, at the sound of a whistle.

15 "Wow," the small lizard yawned, his fatigue overtaking his enthusiasm. "So, how does time work today?" he asked.

16 "The tiniest fractions of seconds matter today; take air travel, for example. It relies on time that is accurate and fixed," I told the young lizard, whose eyes were getting heavier by the moment. "I've even heard some say in this modern era that time does not actually exist."

17 The young lizard began to snore.

18 "Whether we created time or time created us, I know one thing for sure," I whispered. "It is time for bed."

GO ON →

6 **Part A**

What is the meaning of the word **portable** as it is used in paragraph 8?

(A) something that is easy to misplace

(B) something that can be easily carried

(C) something that is based on mathematics

(D) something that can be purchased cheaply

Part B

Which word from paragraph 8 **best** supports the answer to Part A?

(A) captured

(B) refined

(C) accuracy

(D) smaller

7 **Part A**

What does the use of the word **impatiently** in paragraph 9 suggest about the young lizard?

(A) The young lizard is eager to learn more.

(B) The young lizard is in a rush to get on with his day.

(C) The young lizard is confused by the narrator's story.

(D) The young lizard is restless and bored by the narrator's story.

Part B

Which **two** details from the story **best** support the answer to Part A?

(A) "Just as I was about to nap . . ." (paragraph 1)

(B) "I went on for what must have been hours . . ." (paragraph 1)

(C) ". . . the young lizard asked, his tiny jaw nearly hitting the ground." (paragraph 2)

(D) "The little lizard implored me to continue . . ." (paragraph 8)

(E) ". . . the small lizard yawned, his fatigue overtaking . . ." (paragraph 15)

(F) "The young lizard began to snore." (paragraph 17)

GO ON →

8 Select **two** ways that the author's use of first-person narration affects the story, and write them in the chart.

Point of View	Effects on the Story
First-person	

Effects

offers detailed historical information

gives the narrator's thoughts and feelings

stresses the habits and preferences of reptilians

highlights the narrator's unique perspective as a lizard

explains the narrator's relationship with the young lizard

GO ON →

9 **Part A**

Select the statement that **best** explains how the narrator's point of view develops over the course of the story.

(A) In his early years, he is puzzled by time-keeping; later, he starts to understand it.

(B) In his early years, he is entertained by time-keeping; later, he is bored by it.

(C) In his early years, he is uninformed about time-keeping; later, he is shocked by it.

(D) In his early years, he is unappreciative of time-keeping; later, he is enthusiastic about it.

Part B

Which set of sentences from the story **best** supports the answer to Part A?

(A) "I responded with a chuckle and told him that the year I hatched, the calendar to which he referred had not yet been invented." (paragraph 1) / "I was startled when a loud gong blasted through the air; I quite almost lost my tail!" (paragraph 10)

(B) "Though I quite liked the way it looked, I was not a fan of precise methods to track time." (paragraph 7) / "I thought the mechanical clock would be the pinnacle of timepieces—until I met Galileo." (paragraph 12)

(C) "It was odd to me how the humans made plans to meet and disassemble based on the number of gongs." (paragraph 11) / "But alas, time went by and people once again began to prefer smaller clocks and watches." (paragraph 13)

(D) "For a lizard like me, it was a fun form of entertainment." (paragraph 12) / "The little gadgets did not afford me an entertaining ride." (paragraph 13)

GO ON →

10 **Part A**

What theme is **best** developed in the story?

(A) Telling time requires education.

(B) Keeping track of time yields success.

(C) Traveling through time offers unique opportunities.

(D) Society's awareness of time has increased over the years.

Part B

Which sentence from the story **best** supports the answer to Part A?

(A) ". . . time as I knew it fell into two categories: day or night."
(paragraph 5)

(B) "I was startled when a loud gong blasted through the air . . ."
(paragraph 10)

(C) ". . . people once again began to prefer smaller clocks . . ."
(paragraph 13)

(D) "The tiniest fractions of seconds matter today . . ." (paragraph 16)

GO ON →

Today you will read an article and a story about Aztecs.

Read the article "A City of Aztecs." Then answer questions 11 and 12.

A City of Aztecs

1   The Aztec people, who lived hundreds of years ago in today's central Mexico, recorded their history with a pictographic and ideographic writing system. This means they did not use an alphabet to make words and sentences. Instead, they used pictures to represent ideas, and the documents they created looked somewhat like maps.

2   The map-like quality of Aztec documents is appropriate for answering some important questions. Specifically, it helps us understand why the Aztecs settled in the area of modern-day Mexico City. Archeological records show their ancestors came from north of the Colorado River, an area now part of the western United States. They began to move south and arrived in the Valley of Mexico around the year 1200.

3   According to surviving documents, Aztec priests told the people they must keep moving until they saw a special sign. The priests said the sign would be an eagle holding a snake in its mouth and sitting on a cactus. This sign would mark the place to build a glorious city. They searched for the sign for over 100 years. In 1325, a band of Aztecs was resting by a lake called Texcoco when they finally saw the sign. There they built Tenochtitlan, meaning "near the cactus."

4   The Aztecs built Tenochtitlan on a small island in the lake. As the city outgrew the island, more land was made by loading rafts with earth, sinking the rafts, and then piling more earth on top. They then created a complex network of canals, floating gardens, and an excellent water transportation system. They also built pyramids and temples by floating huge stone blocks through canals.

5   When Spanish explorers came to Mexico in 1519, they were amazed by Tenochtitlan. The gleaming city surrounded by a lake resembled a moat around a giant castle. Tenochtitlan, with its bustling markets and impressive pyramids, was home to 250,000 people—three times more people than in any city in Spain. Great bridges and aqueducts connected the city with the rest of the Aztec empire. People traveled miles to visit the markets and brightly painted temples.

GO ON →

6   The pictographic records of the Aztecs are open to interpretation. However, the Spanish records about the Aztecs and Tenochtitlan are quite detailed, and there is little doubt about their meaning. The leader of the explorers, Hernando Cortés, wrote letters to the Spanish king to tell him that capturing Tenochtitlan would bring them great wealth and power.

7   For two years, Cortés formed alliances with other indigenous groups. Cortés and his troops besieged and conquered Tenochtitlan in 1621. The magnificent bridges and causeways leading to the city made it easier to cut off supplies. Cortés quickly tore down most of the Aztec buildings and monuments. The Aztec empire was destroyed. Over its ruins, they began to build a Spanish metropolis in the New World. Today, the ruins of the Templo Mayor are some of the few remnants of the ancient city.

GO ON →

11 **Part A**

The author describes different kinds of written evidence that historians use to answer questions about the history of Tenochtitlan. How does the author show the main difference between Aztec and Spanish records?

Ⓐ by explaining how the Aztec evidence was destroyed, whereas the Spanish evidence was well preserved

Ⓑ by explaining how the Aztecs represented ideas with pictures, whereas the Spanish represented ideas with words

Ⓒ by explaining how the Aztec records were written on stones, whereas the Spanish records were written on paper

Ⓓ by explaining how the Aztec records were written by priests, whereas the Spanish records were written by soldiers

Part B

Which detail from the article **best** supports the answer to Part A?

Ⓐ "The map-like quality of Aztec documents is appropriate for answering some important questions. Specifically, it helps us understand why the Aztecs settled in the area of modern-day Mexico City." (paragraph 2)

Ⓑ "According to surviving documents, the Aztec priests told the people they must keep moving until they saw a special sign. The priests said the sign would be an eagle holding a snake in its mouth and sitting on a cactus." (paragraph 3)

Ⓒ "The pictographic records of the Aztecs are open to interpretation. However, the Spanish records about the Aztecs and Tenochtitlan are quite detailed, and there is little doubt about their meaning." (paragraph 6)

Ⓓ "The Aztec empire was destroyed. Over its ruins, they began to build a Spanish metropolis in the New World." (paragraph 7)

GO ON →

12 The author says that the city of Tenochtitlan outgrew the small island in the middle of Lake Texcoco. How did the Aztecs solve this problem? Use evidence from the article to support your response.

_____

_____

_____

_____

_____

_____

_____

_____

GO ON →

Read the story "Play Ball." Then answer questions 13 and 14.

Play Ball

1 "Coach Gonzales asked me to be the new forward for the Ravens," Sonia muttered, slumping next to her best friend.

2 "All right!" cried Annie, the Ravens' goalie, raising her hand for a celebratory high-five. But Sonia's hand did not meet hers.

3 "What if I don't hear a teammate calling out a play, or the referee blowing a whistle on a foul?" asked Sonia, her apprehension obvious.

4 Annie gently turned Sonia's face toward her. "Do you remember third grade? You asked to sit up front so you could read Ms. Denton's lips more easily. Do you remember what you told her?"

5 "I remember," Sonia responded. "I said that I hear with my eyes."

6 "You'll do that on the field, too," Annie reassured Sonia. Just then, Coach Gonzales arrived.

7 As a strenuous practice concluded, the coach gathered his exhausted players around him. "Team," he said, "if we want to succeed, we have to be good students of the game. I want you all to strive to learn something new about soccer—watch a video of a World Cup championship, or read about the game's history, or ask your parents about the best player they've ever seen. You never know what will give you an advantage." Ducking her head as the redness of her cheeks intensified, Sonia couldn't help but feel that her new coach was speaking directly to her.

8 Exhausted, Sonia drifted asleep reading a book about Aztec sports that Coach Gonzalez had given the team. Around dawn, Sonia dreamed that she was walking to the school soccer field. The bleachers had disappeared, though, and in their place was a large enclosure surrounded by a stone wall covered with intricate carvings of running athletes. The runners wore headbands and strange-looking shorts with leather guards tied at the hips.

9 The field was a narrow, dirt court. A black leather ball rested at the center. Hundreds of spectators stood by the wall, all wearing colorful garments constructed of animal hides, with feathers, beads, and strands of gold or silver woven into extraordinary headdresses.

GO ON →

10 The figures on the carving began to move, forming two distinct teams. The crowd cheered as the teams started—one player leaping to hit the ball with his shoulder, and another knocking it with his leather-padded hip. They players never touched the ball with their hands. And, astonishingly, the ball never touched the ground.

11 Sonia turned to someone next to her. "What game is this?"

12 "It's called *ullamaliztli*. This is the largest court in Tenochtitlan."

13 Sonia watched the game, scrutinizing every detail. The players tried to knock the ball through two stone-carved rings on either side of mid-court. She also observed the players using complex hand signals to communicate with each other. Perhaps they couldn't hear each other over the crowd noise. Sonia waved her arms wildly at a player who looked like Coach Gonzales.

14 The coach was giving Sonia a thumbs-up, when a teammate kicked the ball to him. He leapt up and headed the ball through a ring.

15 Sonia was cheering as her father woke her up.

16 "You have practice today," he said, looking at Sonia so she could read his lips. "Sounds like you've already started."

17 "Oh, no, I was dreaming about this game," said Sonia, laughing. "It wasn't soccer, but you never know what will give you a leg up."

GO ON →

13 **Part A**

Read the sentence from paragraph 8 of the story.

> The bleachers had disappeared, though, and in their place was a large enclosure surrounded by a stone wall covered with intricate carvings of running athletes.

The prefix *en-* means "into." What does the word **enclosure** mean?

(A) a space that is closed in

(B) a space that is closed again

(C) a space that is often closed

(D) a space that is partly closed

Part B

Which word from the sentence **best** helps the reader determine the meaning of the word **enclosure**?

(A) bleachers

(B) disappeared

(C) surrounded

(D) covered

GO ON →

14 **Part A**

How does the author develop Sonia's point of view in the story?

(A) by describing Sonia's frustration that she doesn't have enough time to study the game

(B) by describing Sonia's feelings of self-doubt about being the team's new forward

(C) by describing Sonia's fear that she will no longer be able to rely on her friend

(D) by describing Sonia's shame over the coach criticizing her soccer skills

Part B

Which detail from the story **best** supports the answer to Part A?

(A) "'All right!' cried Annie, the Ravens' goalie, raising her hand for a celebratory high-five. But Sonia's hand did not meet hers." (paragraph 2)

(B) "Ducking her head as the redness of her cheeks intensified, Sonia couldn't help but feel that her new coach was speaking directly to her." (paragraph 7)

(C) "Exhausted, Sonia drifted asleep reading a book about Aztec sports that Coach Gonzalez had given the team." (paragraph 8)

(D) "The coach was giving Sonia a thumbs-up, when a teammate kicked the ball to him." (paragraph 14)

Name: _____ Date: _____

Refer to the article "A City of Aztecs" and the story "Play Ball." Then answer question 15.

15 Both "A City of Aztecs" and "Play Ball" describe several forms of evidence that can be used to learn about the past. Describe these forms of evidence, and explain why some are more reliable than others. Support your answer with examples from **both** the article and the story.

_____

_____

_____

_____

_____

_____

_____

_____

_____

_____

_____

_____

GO ON →

Grade 6 • Unit Assessment • Unit 2

The following passage needs revision. Read the passage. Then answer questions 16 through 25.

My (1) restaurant specializes in pasta. Pasta is an ancient food, but where did it come from? Marco Polo, (2) supposedly brought pasta back to Italy from China in 1925. But 25 years before he returned to China, several pasta (3) were mentioned in printed Italian recipes. So there must have been pasta in Italy before (4) time. Other evidence points to pasta as a food that came from ancient Greece or from Arab lands during the fifth century.

At our restaurant, we have (5) filled with notebooks of special pasta recipes, including some for national holidays. For (6) , we create red and blue pasta with white cheese. Now that's an interesting way to celebrate the Fourth of July and the (7) of American history!

Do you have a favorite pasta dish? Mine is a recipe that calls for three different kinds of (8) . My brother's favorite dish, (9) is made with layers of flat pasta and lots of cheese. In the hot summer (10) , we like to make cold pasta salads with lots of vegetables. We love pasta all year round!

GO ON →

16 Which answer should go in blank (1)?

Ⓐ families

Ⓑ family's

Ⓒ familys'

17 Which answer should go in blank (2)?

Ⓐ an Italian Explorer

Ⓑ an Italian explorer

Ⓒ an Italian explorer,

18 Which answer should go in blank (3)?

Ⓐ dishes

Ⓑ dishies

Ⓒ dishs

19 Which answer should go in blank (4)?

Ⓐ Marco Polos

Ⓑ Marco Polo's

Ⓒ Marco Polos'

20 Which answer should go in blank (5)?

Ⓐ shelf

Ⓑ shelfs

Ⓒ shelves

GO ON →

21 Which answer should go in blank (6)?

Ⓐ Independence day

Ⓑ independence day

Ⓒ Independence Day

22 Which answer should go in blank (7)?

Ⓐ hero

Ⓑ heros

Ⓒ heroes

23 Which answer should go in blank (8)?

Ⓐ fish

Ⓑ fishes

Ⓒ fishies

24 Which answer should go in blank (9)?

Ⓐ (lasagna)

Ⓑ Lasagna

Ⓒ lasagna,

25 Which answer should go in blank (10)?

Ⓐ months

Ⓑ months'

Ⓒ Months

Research Simulation Task

Today you will research the nature and impact of Athens and Sparta, two ancient Greek city-states. You will read one article titled "The Agora of Athens." Then you will read the articles "The Real Winner of the Peloponnesian War" and "Warrior Nation." As you review these sources, you will gather information and answer questions about the impact of Athens and Sparta so you can write an essay.

Read the article titled "The Agora of Athens." Then answer questions 1 through 3.

The Agora of Athens

1   In 1890, workers in Greece were digging a railway trench when they stumbled upon an amazing find: the remains of buildings that dated as far back as 600 BC. Those were the days of ancient Greece; now the ruins lay on the site of the Agora in Athens, Greece's capital city. The Agora, meaning "place of gathering," was the heart of Athenian life. Citizens gathered there to buy goods from merchants and craftsmen. Students flocked there to discuss philosophy with scholars like Plato, Socrates, and Aristotle. Juries sat in judgment at public trials, and citizens elected city officials. People worshipped at altars or gossiped around fountains.

2   In discovering the Agora, workers had unearthed evidence of a powerful and influential society whose legacy has endured through the centuries. As archaeologists excavated the ruins, they began to comprehend the true size of the Agora. The area was large enough to cover several football fields. Eventually, they had to demolish 400 modern buildings to uncover the site.

3   Historians studied the ruins and examined the architecture, sculptures, city plans, and inscriptions. By comparing these finds with ancient writings, they mapped the ruins. Today, people can tour the site in person or online. Most buildings have crumbled to their foundations. Statues display only partial forms. Inscriptions have faded and blurred. Yet each object or stone wall tells a story, piercing the veil of history to illustrate a specific aspect of this great civilization.

4   When citizens first entered the Agora, they came to the two-story Stoa of Attalos, which stretched 381 feet long. (A stoa is a roofed structure like a porch, attached to a building.) It featured 45 marble columns along the outside and 22 along the inside. This building was a center of business and trades. Merchants sold goods and conducted business from 21 rooms located at one end. Reconstructed in the

GO ON →

1950s, the Stoa of Attalos now functions as a museum. Most artifacts are related to the functions of Athenian democracy. These include a water clock that measured time in the courts and bronze ballots used by juries.

5   As citizens left the Stoa of Attalos, they traveled along the Panathenaic Way, a road that stretched diagonally across the agora. Great processions strode down this route. Horsemen trained on its packed gravel surface. Before planners built a stadium in the Agora, the road hosted athletic contests. These included an event that featured full-armored athletes jumping on and off a fast-moving chariot.

6   On their right, citizens could see the Painted Stoa, hung with wooden panels decorated by Athenian artists. These paintings depicted military victories from the mythology and history of Athens. These included the battle of Marathon, the siege and capture of Troy, and the victory over Sparta. A building with no designated function, the Painted Stoa served as a gathering place for citizens.

7   Across the road, the Royal Stoa sat behind a statue of Themis, Goddess of Justice. Copies of city laws were kept here, including those written by the great law-giver, Solon. The laws are carved into wooden *stelae*, or slabs. In front of this building, Socrates and others engaged in famous ethical discussions. Some of these were described in Plato's works.

8   Nearby sat the Old Bouleuterion, which served a council called the *Boule*. With 50 members, the Boule represented the city's main administrative body. Speaking in a council meeting was timed by measuring the flow of water from a clay pot. The Boule prepared business for the Assembly, a body of all adult male citizens that discussed and voted on policy.

9   Next door, the circular Tholos provided office space for government officials. These representatives lived here, or in homes below, ensuring they were always available for public business. The city's official weights and measures were kept in the Tholos.

10 The Heliaia, a square building, served as the courthouse. It contained an open-air, fenced courtyard open to the public. All male citizens took turns serving on juries. Jury size varied, but a jury could contain as many as 500 members. After hearing a case, jurors voted without deliberation, spending little time considering and discussing the case. Majority rule decided verdicts.

GO ON →

11 Finally, citizens would reach the Odeion of Agrippa. This auditorium sat behind six statues of giants and fish-tailed Tritons. Only three of these sculptures have been uncovered by archaeologists. Used for public concerts and events, this auditorium seated about 1,000 people. The hall contained no internal supports and was considered a daring architectural feat for its time.

12 The Agora is not the only relic of the city-state of Athens. Still, its walls and buildings provide concrete physical evidence of the ideals handed down by one of civilization's greatest democracies.

GO ON →

Name: _____ Date: _____

1 **Part A**

Read the sentence from paragraph 2 of the article "The Agora of Athens."

> As archaeologists excavated the ruins, they began to comprehend the true **size** of the Agora.

What does the word **excavated** mean as it is used in the sentence?

(A) cleaned up

(B) studied intently

(C) raised or hoisted

(D) exposed by digging

Part B

Which word from paragraph 2 is a clue to the meaning of **excavated** in Part A?

(A) discovering

(B) unearthed

(C) influential

(D) comprehend

GO ON →

2 **Part A**

What is the author's **main** purpose in "The Agora of Athens"?

(A) to explain how workers accidentally discovered the Agora

(B) to explain what visitors will see when touring the Agora ruins

(C) to describe how the ruins represent Athens's contributions to history

(D) to describe what daily life was like for the citizens of ancient Athens

Part B

Which sentence from the article **best** supports the answer to Part A?

(A) "In 1890, workers in Greece were digging a railway trench when they stumbled upon an amazing find: the remains of buildings that dated as far back as 600 BC." (paragraph 1)

(B) "The Agora, meaning 'place of gathering,' was the heart of Athenian life." (paragraph 1)

(C) "When citizens first entered the Agora, they came to the two-story Stoa of Attalos, which stretched 381 feet long." (paragraph 4)

(D) "Still, its walls and buildings provide concrete physical evidence of the ideals handed down by one of civilization's greatest democracies." (paragraph 12)

GO ON →

Name: _____ Date: _____

3 The author describes the different structures in the Agora. Next to each structure listed below, write **one** idea that it reveals about ancient Athenian society. Then write **one** piece of evidence that supports **each** idea.

Agora Structure	Idea	Evidence
Stoa of Attalos		
Old Bouleuterion		
The Heliaia		

Ideas:
Athletic games kept Athenians fit in both body and mind.
Athens was a democracy governed by its citizens.
Trade and commerce flourished in Athens.
Athens honored its philosophers and celebrated its warriors.
Citizen juries administered justice according to Athens's laws.

Evidence:
- "Merchants sold goods and conducted business from 21 rooms located at one end." (paragraph 4)
- "These included an event that featured full-armored athletes jumping on and off a fast-moving chariot." (paragraph 5)
- "These paintings depicted military victories from the mythology and history of Athens." (paragraph 6)
- "The Boule prepared business for the Assembly, a body of all adult male citizens that discussed and voted on policy." (paragraph 8)
- "After hearing a case, jurors voted without deliberation, spending little time considering and discussing the case." (paragraph 10)

GO ON →

Read the article "The Real Winner of the Peloponnesian War." Then answer questions 4 through 6.

The Real Winner of the Peloponnesian War

1   In ancient Greece, two city-states stood out from the rest: Athens and Sparta. Constantly at war, these civilizations were bitter rivals. Most of their battles took place during the Peloponnesian War (431–404 BC). Even though Sparta technically won the war, Athens emerged as the most important and influential city in ancient Greece.

2   The societies of Sparta and Athens were organized around vastly different principles. The values of each city-state affected its education, culture, and the opportunities offered its citizens.

3   The Spartan city-state was centered around military power. For boys, military training began at age seven, when they left their families to live in army barracks. Men served in the army until age sixty. Even if they married, men's lives continued to center on the army, and they did not live with their wives. Girls were also required to become fit and strong so they could give birth to healthy babies—especially boys who would become soldiers.

4   In Athens, life had a different focus. Rather than training for war, Athenian children were educated to become thinkers. At around age six, boys were sent to private schools, where they learned arithmetic and read important Greek works. They also wrestled, practiced military skills, and developed artistic talents, like singing and playing the lyre. As a result, Athenian boys had a well-rounded education that included knowing how to fight. After finishing their education, Athenians served a two-year stint in the army. Although they could be called back to the army until age sixty, they were free to pursue other ambitions.

5   So, the ideals most valued by Athens and Sparta determined the quality of life in each city-state. These values also affected how history remembers each society. Spartans are viewed as valiant warriors, with examples like King Leonidas, King Agis, and King Cleomene. Today, people use the adjective *spartan* to refer to someone who is strict, sternly disciplined, and lives plainly. Athenians, however, are remembered for establishing a democratic society, developing principles of justice, and promoting philosophy and the arts. The philosophers Plato, Socrates, and Aristotle were all Athenians. Ironically, so is one of the most famous warriors in history, Alexander the Great.

GO ON →

6 Despite the fact that Athenians' lives did not center on the military, Athens actually started more wars than Sparta. Often, Sparta waited for other city-states to start conflicts before swooping in to gain a military advantage. On the other hand, Athens had a different strategy: the expansion of its city-state. After Athens annexed a new state, it took direct control over its citizens by installing Athenian officials in government positions. Sparta, however, took a different approach, choosing not to directly govern conquered states. Instead, they enslaved local citizens and put them to work farming and providing goods for Sparta's army. This approach had negative consequences. While Sparta focused on strengthening its army, Athens continued to widen its influence in the region, thereby increasing the population of educated, free citizens.

7 Today, not much is left of Sparta. The city of Athens, however, still exists, as does its impact on the world today. For example, the idea of democratic government came from Athens, with principles that have inspired movements throughout the world, including both the French and American Revolutions. Ancient Athenians also made major contributions to math, science, philosophy, and art. Athens may have surrendered to Sparta during the Peloponnesian War, but in the battle to affect history, Athens remains the victor.

GO ON →

4 **Part A**

What does the word **annexed** mean as it is used in paragraph 6 of "The Real Winner of the Peloponnesian War"?

(A) absorbed new territory

(B) destroyed in battle

(C) improved upon

(D) settled into

Part B

Which detail from paragraph 6 **best** supports the answer to Part A?

(A) ". . . started more wars than Sparta."

(B) ". . . waited for other city-states to start conflicts . . ."

(C) ". . . the expansion of its city-state."

(D) ". . . installing Athenian officials in government positions."

GO ON →

5 **Part A**

The author makes the claim that the values of Athens and Sparta helped determine the influence of each city-state. Which strategy does the author use to develop this claim?

(A) The author explains a problem faced by Athens and Sparta and then presents a solution.

(B) The author presents ideas and details about Athens and Sparta in order of importance.

(C) The author compares and contrasts the ideals and actions of Athens and Sparta.

(D) The author sorts facts about Athens and Sparta into different categories.

Part B

Which **two** sentences from the article **best** support the answer to Part A?

(A) "Most of their battles took place during the Peloponnesian War (431–404 BC)." (paragraph 1)

(B) "The Spartan city-state was centered around military power." (paragraph 3)

(C) "Men served in the army until age sixty." (paragraph 3)

(D) "Rather than training for war, Athenian children were educated to become thinkers." (paragraph 4)

(E) "Spartans are viewed as valiant warriors, with examples like King Leonidas, King Agis, and King Cleomene." (paragraph 5)

(F) "Often, Sparta waited for other city-states to start conflicts before swooping in to gain a military advantage." (paragraph 6)

GO ON →

6 **Part A**

Which statement **best** states how paragraph 7 of "The Real Winner of the Peloponnesian War" contributes to the article?

(A) It explains what is physically left of Sparta.

(B) It explains what is physically left of Athens.

(C) It explains how Athens surrendered to Sparta.

(D) It explains why Athens actually won the war.

Part B

Which detail from paragraph 7 **best** supports the answer to Part A?

(A) "Today, not much is left of Sparta."

(B) "The city of Athens, however, still exists . . ."

(C) ". . . as does its impact on the world today."

(D) "Athens may have surrendered to Sparta . . ."

GO ON →

Read the article "Warrior Nation." Then answer questions 7 and 8.

Warrior Nation

1   Sparta was one of the most famous cities in ancient Greece. Located on the banks of the Eurotas River, it was founded by Lacedaemon, who named it after his wife. Sparta was as powerful and important as she was beautiful. She inspired her country's soldiers, who marched into battle shouting her name. The city of Sparta became known for producing generations of warriors.

2   Spartan kings led their warriors to protect the city and vanquish the surrounding kingdoms. Around 700 BC, the Spartans conquered Messenia. After this victory, Sparta went beyond taking the land, enslaving its people and calling them "helots." To strengthen its army, Sparta tasked the helots with farming the land in Sparta and other conquered areas. Although helots provided food for Spartan citizens, Spartans treated them poorly, subjecting them to the whip, and withholding food. Some Spartans even killed helots who seemed too smart or fit, depriving the slaves of potential leaders and keeping them under control.

3   Sparta's actions had one central purpose: to strengthen the military and create the best soldiers in all of Greece. Government policy focused on training boys to become warriors. At seven years old, boys headed to the Agoge for training in military life. There, the boys were required to fight one another and participate in other mock battles to prepare them for the hardships of war. The most skilled soldiers became members of the Crypteia, a special police force designed to watch over and punish the helots. Everyone else joined the army, devoting their lives to protecting Sparta and building it into a powerful city-state.

4   As a result of its military focus, Sparta made significant gains, with many Greek city-states fearing to meet the Spartans in battle. However, other city-states like Athens decided to take on the Spartans. They were challenged, in part, by the prospect of capturing Spartan warriors—an impressive feat that could bring much glory. For years, the Spartans managed to avoid total defeat. During the Peloponnesian War, the Athenians came close, winning a few battles, but eventually losing the war. However, that would be Sparta's last major victory.

5   Ten years after the end of the Peloponnesian War, Thebes—along with Corinth, Athens, and Argos—challenged Sparta. In the war that followed, Sparta finally paid a price for mistreating the helots when these slaves revolted, and joined the enemy. The allied Theban forces fought hard, costing the Spartans more than 4,000 warriors. In just a few short years, the city-state of Sparta—one of the most powerful in Greece—fell for good.

GO ON →

7 **Part A**

Read the sentence from paragraph 2 of "Warrior Nation."

> Spartan kings led their warriors to protect the city and vanquish the surrounding kingdoms.

What is the meaning of the word **vanquish** as it is used in the sentence?

(A) defeat in battle

(B) compete with

(C) criticize rivals

(D) seize enemy soldiers

Part B

Which word from paragraph 2 is a clue to the meaning of **vanquish** in Part A?

(A) protect

(B) conquered

(C) tasked

(D) provided

GO ON →

8 **Part A**

How does paragraph 2 contribute to the development of ideas in "Warrior Nation"?

(A) It illustrates one of the practices that led to Sparta's eventual defeat.

(B) It explains the role of Spartan kings in leading their armies.

(C) It suggests that the helots were too smart to remain slaves.

(D) It shows why conquering Messenia was easy for Sparta.

Part B

Which **two** sentences from the article **best** support the answer to Part A?

(A) "The city of Sparta became known for producing generations of warriors." (paragraph 1)

(B) "Around 700 BC, the Spartans conquered Messenia." (paragraph 2)

(C) "Although helots provided food for Spartan citizens, Spartans treated them poorly, subjecting them to the whip, and withholding food." (paragraph 2)

(D) "Sparta's actions had one central purpose: to strengthen the military and create the best soldiers in all of Greece." (paragraph 3)

(E) "The most skilled soldiers became members of the Crypteia, a special police force designed to watch over and punish the helots." (paragraph 3)

(F) "In the war that followed, Sparta finally paid a price for mistreating the helots when these slaves revolted, and joined the enemy." (paragraph 5)

GO ON →

Refer to the articles "The Agora of Athens," "The Real Winner of the Peloponnesian War," and "Warrior Nation." Then answer questions 9 and 10.

9 Mark **one** central idea that is developed in all three articles. Then circle **one** sentence from **each** article that supports the central idea.

Central Idea
_____ Sparta's warrior culture affected its citizens from a young age.
_____ Athens and Sparta had different policies toward the populations of conquered states.
_____ Education and democratic ideals are more influential than violence and aggression.
_____ Both major Greek city-states produced armies of brave warriors.

"The Agora of Ancient Athens"	"The Real Winner of the Peloponnesian War"	"Warrior Nation"
"As archaeologists excavated the ruins, they began to comprehend the true size of the Agora."	"The societies of Sparta and Athens were organized around vastly different principles."	"The city of Sparta became known for producing generations of warriors."
"These included an event that featured full-armored athletes jumping on and off a fast-moving chariot."	"Even if they married, men's lives continued to center on the army, and they did not live with their wives."	"Sparta was one of the most famous cities in ancient Greece."
"This auditorium sat behind six statues of giants and fish-tailed Tritons."	"At around age six, boys were sent to private schools, where they learned arithmetic and read important Greek works."	"As a result of its military focus, Sparta made significant gains, with many Greek city-states fearing to meet the Spartans . . ."
"Still, its walls and buildings provide concrete physical evidence of the ideals handed down by one of civilization's greatest democracies."	"For example, the idea of democratic government came from Athens, with principles that have inspired movements throughout the world . . ."	"During the Peloponnesian War, the Athenians came close, winning a few battles, but eventually losing the war."

GO ON →

10 You have read three sources that claim that Athens was a more influential city-state than Sparta. Write an essay that compares and contrasts the evidence each source uses to support this claim. Be sure to use evidence from all **three** sources to support your response.

Write your essay on a separate sheet of paper.

STOP

Answer Key

Name: _____

Question	Correct Answer	Content Focus	CCSS	Complexity
1A	C	Personification	RI.6.1, RI.6.4, L.6.5a	DOK 2
1B	A	Personification	RI.6.1, RI.6.4, L.6.5a	DOK 2
2A	C	Greek and Latin Prefixes	RI.6.1, RI.6.4, L.6.4b	DOK 2
2B	C, F	Greek and Latin Prefixes	RI.6.1, RI.6.4, L.6.4b	DOK 2
3A	D	Text Structure: Compare and Contrast	RI.6.1, RI.6.5	DOK 2
3B	A	Text Structure: Compare and Contrast	RI.6.1, RI.6.5	DOK 2
4	see below	Text Structure: Problem and Solution	RI.6.1, RI.6.5	DOK 2
5	see below	Text Feature: Timeline	RI.6.1, RI.6.7	DOK 1
6A	B	Latin Roots	RL.6.1, RL.6.4, L.6.4b	DOK 2
6B	D	Latin Roots	RL.6.1, RL.6.4, L.6.4b	DOK 2
7A	A	Connotation and Denotation	RL.6.1, RL.6.4, L.6.5c	DOK 2
7B	C, D	Connotation and Denotation	RL.6.1, RL.6.4, L.6.5c	DOK 2
8	see below	Point of View	RL.6.1, RL.6.6	DOK 3
9A	D	Point of View	RL.6.1, RL.6.6	DOK 3
9B	B	Point of View	RL.6.1, RL.6.6	DOK 2
10A	D	Theme	RL.6.1, RL.6.2	DOK 3
10B	D	Theme	RL.6.1, RL.6.2	DOK 2
11A	B	Text Structure: Compare and Contrast	RI.6.1, RI.6.5	DOK 2
11B	C	Text Structure: Compare and Contrast	RI.6.1, RI.6.5	DOK 2
12	see below	Text Structure: Problem and Solution	RI.6.1, RI.6.5	DOK 2
13A	A	Greek and Latin Prefixes	RL.6.1, RL.6.4, L.6.4b	DOK 2
13B	C	Greek and Latin Prefixes	RL.6.1, RL.6.4, L.6.4b	DOK 2
14A	B	Point of View	RL.6.1, RL.6.6	DOK 3

Answer Key

Name: _____

Question	Correct Answer	Content Focus	CCSS	Complexity
14B	B	Point of View	RL.6.1, RL.6.6	DOK 2
15	see below	Compare Across Texts	W.6.9	DOK 4
16	B	Possessive Nouns	L.6.1	DOK 1
17	C	Appositives	L.6.2a	DOK 1
18	A	Singular and Plural Nouns	L.6.1	DOK 1
19	B	Possessive Nouns	L.6.1	DOK 1
20	C	Singular and Plural Nouns	L.6.1	DOK 1
21	C	Kinds of Nouns	L.6.1	DOK 1
22	C	More Plural Nouns	L.6.1	DOK 1
23	A	More Plural Nouns	L.6.1	DOK 1
24	C	Appositives	L.6.2a	DOK 1
25	A	Kinds of Nouns	L.6.1	DOK 1

Comprehension: Selected Response 3A, 3B, 4, 5, 8, 9A, 9B, 10A, 10B, 11A, 11B, 14A, 14B	/16	%
Comprehension: Constructed Response 12, 15	/6	%
Vocabulary 1A, 1B, 2A, 2B, 6A, 6B, 7A, 7B, 13A, 13B	/10	%
English Language Conventions 16-25	/10	%
Total Unit Assessment Score	/42	%

4 Students should write "by showing how the Pilgrims overcame problems" in the **Strategy** box and "The entire group squeezed onto one ship and spent 65 days at sea" and "The Pilgrims attempted to live in Plymouth despite bad weather and lack of food" in the **Details** boxes.

5 Students should write the following numbers: 2, 1, 3, 6, 4, 5.

8 Students should write "gives the narrator's thoughts and feelings" and "highlights the narrator's unique perspective as a lizard" in the chart.

12 **2-point response:** The Aztecs made their island city bigger by using rafts piled up with earth. They let the rafts sink along the shores of the island. When the piles of rafts and earth rose above the water surface, the island became larger. They also built bridges to connect the island to the rest of the Aztec empire.

15 **4-point response:** Many forms of evidence can provide opportunities for learning about the past. For example, "A City of Aztecs" discusses the pictographic writing system of the Aztecs. Instead of using an alphabet, the Aztecs used pictures. "Play Ball" also mentions the carvings of the Aztecs. Images like these help us understand why the Aztecs settled in modern-day Mexico City and built Tenochtitlan on the island in Lake Texcoco.

Other forms of evidence include the physical remains of cities. The Aztecs constructed a network of canals, floating gardens, and a water transportation system. But only ruins of one temple still exist to study. In "Play Ball," Sonia reads a book about the Aztecs, which is likely based on careful research. She learns that the Aztecs built the largest ullamaliztli court in Tenochtitlan next to a great pyramid to honor their gods. The story also references the costumes the Aztecs wore, which we probably know about through drawings and carvings.

Some forms of evidence are more reliable than others. As "A City of Aztecs" mentions, the pictographic writing system leaves room for interpretation. The Spanish left behind many written accounts using words, though, so there is little doubt as to their meaning. Written accounts such as the one Cortés wrote to the Spanish King are very reliable.

Name: _____

Unit 2 Assessment: Research Simulation Task

Question	Answer	CCSS	Complexity
1A	D	RI.6.1, RI.6.4, L.6.4a	DOK 2
1B	B		DOK 2
2A	C	RI.6.1, RI.6.6	DOK 3
2B	D		DOK 2
3	see below	RI.6.1, RI.6.5	DOK 2
4A	A	RI.6.1, RI.6.4, L.6.4a	DOK 2
4B	C		DOK 2
5A	C	RI.6.1, RI.6.8	DOK 2
5B	B, D		DOK 2
6A	D	RI.6.1, RI.6.3, RI.6.5	DOK 2
6B	C		DOK 2
7A	A	RI.6.1, RI.6.4, L.6.4a	DOK 2
7B	B		DOK 2
8A	A	RI.6.1, RI.6.5	DOK 3
8B	C, F		DOK 2
9	see below	RI.6.1, RI.6.2	DOK 2
10	see below	RI.6.1, RI.6.8, RI.6.9 W.6.2, W.6.4–W.6.10 L.6.1, L.6.2, L.6.3, L.6.6	DOK 4

Comprehension 2A, 2B, 3, 5A, 5B, 6A, 6B, 8A, 8B, 9	/12	%
Vocabulary 1A, 1B, 4A, 4B, 7A, 7B	/6	%
Prose Constructed Response 10	/4 [RC] /12 [WE] /3 [LC]	%
Total Research Simulation Score	/37	%

3 Students should complete the chart as follows:
Stoa of Attalos—Idea: Trade and commerce flourished in Athens. Evidence: "Merchants sold goods and conducted business from 21 rooms located at one end." (paragraph 4); Old Bouleuterion—Idea: Athens was a democracy governed by its citizens. Evidence: "The Boule prepared business for the Assembly, a body of all adult male citizens that discussed and voted on policy." (paragraph 8); The Heliaia—Idea: Citizen juries administered justice according to Athens's laws. Evidence: "After hearing a case, jurors voted without deliberation, spending little time considering and discussing the case." (paragraph 10)

9 Students should mark/circle the following answers:
Central Idea: Education and democratic ideals are more influential than violence and aggression; "The Agora of Ancient Athens": "Still, its walls and buildings provide concrete physical evidence of the ideals handed down by one of civilization's greatest democracies." (paragraph 12); "The Real Winner of the Peloponnesian War": ". . . the idea of democratic government came from Athens, with principles that have inspired movements throughout the world, including both the French and American Revolutions." (paragraph 7); "Warrior Nation": "The city of Sparta became known for producing generations of warriors." (paragraph 1)

10 **19-point anchor paper:**

Athens and Sparta were two of ancient Greece's most powerful city-states. The ideals and actions of these cities were quite different. While Sparta built a warrior society, Athens emphasized education, democracy, and the arts, and fought to expand the population of free citizens throughout Greece.

In "The Agora of Athens," the author describes the ruins of this gathering place and explains what the ancient structures illustrate about the society of this Greek city-state. In paragraph 1, the author states that the Agora "was the heart of Athenian life." Citizens bought and sold goods in the Stoa of Attalos, the center of business and trade. In describing the Royal Stoa, the author notes that this building represented the Greek idea of justice, which inspired many future societies. Inside were laws carved into wooden slabs. Nearby, the Heliaia functioned as the courthouse. The author notes that "All male citizens took turns serving on juries," another tradition that has endured. Representing citizen rule was the Old Bouleuterion, where a council body prepared business for the Assembly, where all citizens voted on policy. The author also mentions an auditorium, a public way, and gathering places—evidence that Athenians placed great value on education, arts, sports, and philosophy. The structures within the Agora reflect the ideals of ancient Athens, evidence of their powerful and lasting impact.

In "The Real Winner of the Peloponnesian War," the author compares and contrasts Athens and Sparta, arguing that although Sparta was the victor, Athens actually gained more power and influence. In paragraph 2, the author states, "The values of each city-state affected its education, culture, and the opportunities offered its citizens." Spartan society was centered on military power, with boys leaving their families to train for the army. In contrast, although Athenian boys received military training, "Athenian children were trained to become thinkers." Athenians received a well-rounded education, and produced influential philosophers like Plato, Socrates, and Aristotle. The author also compares how each city-state treated the people in its conquered states. Sparta enslaved whole populations to provide for its army, and treated slaves harshly. Athens, however, brought in its own officials to administer governments and spread its values. So while Sparta created slaves who would later turn against them, Athens was increasing the number of free citizens. Finally, the author explains that not much is left of Sparta today, although it is remembered for its fierce warriors. In contrast, Athens helped spread the idea of democracy.

In "Warrior Nation," the author details how Sparta arose as a city of warriors and shows how their ideals and actions eventually weakened it. For example, in paragraph 2, the author states that when Sparta conquered Messina, "Sparta went beyond taking the land, enslaving its people and calling them "helots." Then they made them work to produce food and other goods for its army. They also mistreated them, "subjecting them to the whip, and withholding food. Some Spartans even killed helots who seemed too smart or fit, depriving the slaves of potential leaders and keeping them under control." While Sparta's military focus strengthened it for a time, after winning many battles, it emerged in a weaker position. Thebes allied with other cities, including Athens, to challenge Sparta. The helots revolted, also joining the allied forces, who defeated Sparta. With this evidence, the author shows how focusing on military victories failed to build Sparta's influence. While people remember their warriors, little else about Sparta has endured.

Read the story "Saving the Po'ouli." Then answer questions 1 through 5.

Saving the Po'ouli

1 Everyone knew where to find 12-year-old Billy van der Merven. Don't look on the soccer field, or in front of the TV. Don't bother looking in his bedroom.

2 "Go look in the forest behind the house," his mother would say. "He'll be out there with a bird book in one hand and a pair of binoculars in the other." Billy had been interested in birds for as long as he could remember. His mother loved telling people that Billy's first word was not "Mama" or "Dada." It was "bird."

3 His interest in birds lasted all the way through school, until he graduated from college and shortened his name to the more adult-sounding "Bill." In 1998, Bill traveled to Hawaii as a tourist. He went straight to one of the best places for seeing unusual bird species—the rainy, steep slopes of Haleakala volcano on Maui. Bill had done his homework with his characteristic intensity. He had a long checklist of rare birds he hoped to see. Many had strange, poetic Hawaiian names, like the Akepa, the I'iwi, and the Kiwikiu. Others had typically descriptive names like the Maui Parrotbill or the Wandering Tattler. But the bird he most wanted to see was the Po'ouli.

4 Some people called the Po'ouli the black-faced honeycreeper, but Bill preferred the Hawaiian name because the bird was found only in Hawaii. The Po'ouli was one of the rarest birds in the world. Bill thought of it—a stout little brown bird with a black bandit's mask—as the Lone Ranger of the bird world. The Po'ouli had been discovered only 25 years before by a group of university students. At the time, there were as few as 200 individuals, and each year that small number went down at an alarming rate.

5 To help him find and identify the birds on his checklist, Bill arranged for a guide. Leilani was a ranger at Haleakala National Park and an expert naturalist. She showed Bill around the park, helping him with the vowel-heavy Hawaiian names and identifying many birds by their distinct calls. Bill had spent many years in the forest and had a good eye for spotting birds, but Leilani made him feel blind. She could see birds, insects, footprints, and other animal signs that he would have simply walked past.

6 As Leilani guided Bill through the forest, it quickly became clear that the Po'ouli's habitat was severely threatened. She pointed out the telltale signs of invasive animals like pigs, snakes, rats, and mongooses. All of these animals were

GO ON →

transported to Hawaii by ships from Europe, America, or Asia. They thrived in the warm, wet environment in Hawaii, and the native animals had no defenses against them. Even insects were part of the problem. When Bill swatted mosquitoes, she explained that they bore non-native diseases that killed many local birds.

7   She pointed to a snail and said, "That's a Rosy wolfsnail, or 'cannibal snail.' When the African land snail was brought to Hawaii on cargo ships, it started to eat rice and other crops. So, this snail was introduced to eat the African invader. Unfortunately, the Rosy decided it liked the taste of Hawaiian snails better, so it quickly climbed the mountains and wiped out 20 native species of snails."

8   "That's awful," said Bill.

9   "Yes, it is," Leilani agreed. "One of the native species the Rosy wolfsnail really loves is the Kahuli tree snail. And guess which bird depends on that snail for food?"

10 "Don't tell me," said Bill. "The Po'ouli." Leilani nodded with a sad frown.

11 Bill looked around him at the beautiful forest. It was alive with birds and prehistoric-looking plants. It didn't look like an ecosystem under threat. But now he knew the truth. He had come to Hawaii with the goal of simply *seeing* a Po'ouli. In that instant, his goal changed to saving them.

12 Bill remained in Hawaii. He found a small home close to Haleakala National Park and joined many academic and scientific teams that traveled deep into the park to search for the Po'ouli and other endangered species.

13 The story of the Po'ouli ended sadly. Bill was part of a team that caught one of the last three individuals in 2004, in an effort to capture a breeding pair. Before another could be caught, the old male Po'ouli died in captivity. No one has seen the other two for over 10 years, and the species is believed to be extinct.

14 Today, Bill van der Merven is well-known for his tireless efforts to protect the Haleakala rainforest. When he's not in the forest watching his beloved birds, he is working with habitat protection groups, fencing off large sections of the forest, raising funds, writing articles, and arranging creative partnerships between the government and funding organizations. He knows that even if there are no more living Po'ouli, his efforts will help 31 other endangered bird species in Hawaii. But he never wavers in his optimistic belief that the Po'ouli will survive.

GO ON →

Name: _____ Date: _____

1 Select the correct meanings of the words **unusual** and **intensity** as they are used in paragraph 3, and write them in the chart.

unusual	
intensity	

Meanings

state of determination	commonplace	not familiar
unexceptional	moderate nature	quality of laziness

2 **Part A**

Read the sentence from paragraph 14.

> But he never wavers in his optimistic belief that the Po'ouli will survive.

Which word has almost the same meaning as **optimistic**?

(A) doubtful   (C) realistic

(B) educated   (D) positive

Part B

Why does the narrator use the word **optimistic** to describe Bill's belief that the species will survive?

(A) The Po'ouli has not been seen in a decade and is likely extinct.

(B) Bill and his team were unable to save the old male Po'ouli they captured.

(C) Bill is an expert in the field and has been researching rare birds since the '90s.

(D) The government and other organizations work with Bill to help many endangered bird species.

GO ON →

3 Read the sentence from paragraph 4.

> Bill thought of it—a stout little brown bird with a black bandit's mask—as the Lone Ranger of the bird world.

Why does the narrator explain that Bill thinks of the Po'ouli as "the Lone Ranger of the bird world"? Select **two** options.

(A) It shows that Bill cares deeply about the bird.

(B) It reminds the reader that the Po'ouli is extremely rare.

(C) It reveals how challenging it is to locate the Po'ouli in the wild.

(D) It proves the reader's suspicion that the Po'ouli is endangered.

(E) It suggests that the Po'ouli steals its food from other bird species.

(F) It provides a specific image of what Bill believes the Po'ouli looks like.

4 **Part A**

What message does the author want the reader to understand in paragraph 6?

(A) The Po'ouli is native to Hawaii.

(B) The forest shows signs of activity.

(C) The forest is a very delicate habitat.

(D) Many species live on multiple continents.

Part B

Which sentence from the story **best** supports the answer to Part A?

(A) "Some people called the Po'ouli the black-faced honeycreeper, but Bill preferred the Hawaiian name because the bird was found only in Hawaii." (paragraph 4)

(B) "'When the African land snail was brought to Hawaii on cargo ships, it started to eat rice and other crops.'" (paragraph 7)

(C) "'Unfortunately, the Rosy decided it liked the taste of Hawaiian snails better, so it quickly climbed the mountains and wiped out 20 native species of snails.'" (paragraph 7)

(D) "It was alive with birds and prehistoric-looking plants." (paragraph 11)

GO ON →

5 **Part A**

What theme is **best** developed in the story "Saving the Po'ouli"?

(A) Humans do more harm than good when they interfere with delicate ecosystems.

(B) Saving an endangered species requires a lot of knowledge and hard work.

(C) Trying to save an endangered species is a hopeless pursuit.

(D) Finding a job one loves is more difficult than it sounds.

Part B

Which paragraph **best** supports the answer to Part A?

(A) paragraph 6

(B) paragraph 11

(C) paragraph 13

(D) paragraph 14

GO ON →

Read the article "Surviving the South Pole." Then answer questions 6 through 10.

Surviving the South Pole

1   In 1915, a British explorer named Ernest Shackleton led a team of explorers to Antarctica. Their goal was to cross the continent, passing through the South Pole along the way. Though Shackleton had come very close on two previous expeditions, he would not be the first person to reach the South Pole. That extraordinary feat had been accomplished only four years earlier by a Norwegian explorer named Roald Amundsen.

2   Shackleton convinced the British government and his business partners that crossing the entire Antarctic by foot was the last, great challenge of the Age of Discovery. His plan was to land two ships on either side of the continent. One ship would carry an overland crew of 28 men. The other would place food and equipment along the tail end of the route.

3   Shackleton led the overland group, which sailed aboard the *Endurance*. It was a sturdy wooden ship with strong oak beams over four feet thick at the front. However, the *Endurance* was no match for the drifting ice fields off the Antarctic coast. Less than two months into their journey, the ship was trapped in a crushing field of ice almost 200 miles from their intended destination. Shackelton recognized the danger and told his crew to prepare for a long wait. He hoped that the wind would change direction and loosen the ice around the ship. After several near escapes, the ice closed in and broke through the walls of the *Endurance*. The crew was ordered to abandon ship and make camp on the ice for the time being.

4   It was clear to all members of the expedition that the original goal of crossing the Antarctic was lost. Camping on the ice far from their planned landing point, the only objective was survival. This would not be an easy task. Supplies were very low, fuel for fires was limited, the weather alternated between freezing winds and warm, slushy periods that left clothing and sleeping bags wet and uncomfortable. The *Endurance* finally sank 11 months after it was first trapped in the ice. The crew had removed every useful thing from the ship, including many photographic plates taken by the expedition's photographer, Frank Hurley. One famous photo shows the *Endurance* at night, ghostly and forlorn in a sea of ice.

GO ON →

5   Shackleton then made the difficult decision to move their makeshift camp to a nearby island. He hoped they might be able to signal a passing whaling ship to rescue them. Cold and exhausted, the crew slowly dragged three lifeboats across a dangerous, shifting landscape of icebergs and melting islands of ice. On several occasions, scouting parties were attacked by 13-foot long, 1,000-pound leopard seals. They made slow progress for a few weeks, but it was no use. The ice was drifting faster than they could travel by foot. Finally, there was not enough solid ice to stand on, so the crew loaded their remaining supplies into the lifeboats and set off for the nearest island. Wind and currents pushed them wildly around the Weddell Sea, until at last they landed on Elephant Island. This lonely, isolated rock offered no hope of rescue. It was far from the shipping routes, and the ferocity of the high winds would make it difficult for any rescue boat to reach the shore. But the crew was thankful that they had at least regained solid ground. They had been floating on the ice for over a year.

6   With very few supplies and another harsh winter approaching, Shackleton decided he must go for help. He and five crew members sailed a 20-foot lifeboat 720 miles through stormy seas to South Georgia Island. In heavy seas, they took turns chopping the ice off the ropes with an axe so that the added weight did not sink their tiny boat. Experienced sailors regularly cite this journey as one of the greatest seafaring accomplishments in history.

7   But Shackleton's ordeal was not over yet. He and his companions had made it to South Georgia, but the whaling station was on the other side of the island. They couldn't risk another sea voyage. So, Shackleton and two companions hiked 32 miles over an icy mountain pass to the whaling station. From there, he organized an expedition back to Elephant Island to collect his crew. They had been living at the windswept camp for over four months. Most believed that Shackleton had died during his attempt to find help on South Georgia Island. The crew of the *Endurance* was finally rescued 20 months after they began their journey. Everyone had survived.

8   To this day, Shackleton's expedition is considered one of the greatest accomplishments in the history of polar exploration. Though he did not achieve his original goal of traveling overland across Antarctica, Shackleton's leadership in the face of extreme hazards, and the fact that all 28 crew members survived the ordeal, was remarkable. One hundred years later, it's difficult to imagine the hardships Shackleton and his crew endured. They had no modern technologies to rely on. There were no radios, telephones, or satellite navigation systems. Theirs were the most basic tools for survival: persistence, bravery, teamwork, leadership, and a positive attitude.

GO ON →

Name: _____ Date: _____

6 **Part A**

Read the sentence from paragraph 5.

> Shackleton then made the difficult decision to move their makeshift camp to a nearby island.

Which **two** words are antonyms of **makeshift**?

(A) contained

(B) simple

(C) permanent

(D) reserved

(E) stable

(F) precious

Part B

Which detail from the article **best** helps the reader to determine the meaning of the word **makeshift**?

(A) ". . . for the time being." (paragraph 3)

(B) ". . . that left clothing and sleeping bags wet and uncomfortable." (paragraph 4)

(C) ". . . might be able to signal a passing whaling ship . . ." (paragraph 5)

(D) ". . . was far from the shipping routes . . ." (paragraph 5)

Copyright © McGraw-Hill Education

GO ON →

7 Select the correct meanings of the words **ferocity**, **thankful**, and **regained** as they are used in paragraph 5. Write the meanings on the lines next to the words.

ferocity _____

thankful _____

regained _____

Meanings

made from iron	increased in amount	a violent quality
lacking in gratitude	something gotten again	filled with appreciation

GO ON →

Name: _____ Date: _____

8 Draw lines to connect each effect to its cause or causes. Not all causes will be used.

Cause	Effect

Cause

Supplies, such as fuel for fires, were low.

The ship was made of sturdy oak beams that were four feet thick.

The crew learned that Amundsen had beaten them to the South Pole.

The ship was trapped a long distance away from the planned landing point.

The crew removed photographs of the ship when they abandoned it.

The *Endurance* got stuck in a field of ice.

Ice broke through the walls of the *Endurance*.

Effect

Shackleton ordered his crew to prepare for a long wait.

The objective of the Shackleton expedition changed to survival.

GO ON →

9 **Part A**

Which statement **best** summarizes the central idea of the article?

(A) Antarctica is not a continent fit for humans.

(B) Shackleton was not embarrassed to admit defeat.

(C) Polar explorers must be prepared to handle any situation.

(D) Shackleton's journey is a historic example of endurance.

Part B

Which detail from the article **best** supports the answer to Part A?

(A) "On several occasions, scouting parties were attacked by 13-foot long, 1,000-pound leopard seals. They made slow progress for a few weeks, but it was no use." (paragraph 5)

(B) "He and his companions had made it to South Georgia, but the whaling station was on the other side of the island. They couldn't risk another sea voyage." (paragraph 7)

(C) "The crew of the *Endurance* was finally rescued 20 months after they began their journey. Everyone had survived." (paragraph 7)

(D) "They had no modern technologies to rely on. There were no radios, telephones, or satellite navigation systems." (paragraph 8)

GO ON →

10 How does the sequential text structure of the article add to the reader's understanding of Shackleton's expedition? Support your answer with details from the article.

_____

_____

_____

_____

_____

_____

_____

GO ON →

Today you will read a story and an article about overcoming challenges.

Read the story "Blind Racer." Then answer questions 11 and 12.

Blind Racer

1 The sun shines brightly over Mount Hood, Oregon, making the new snow gleam a brilliant white. At the summit, a lone skier, 12-year-old Evie McQueen, feels the warmth of the sun on her face and smiles at the prospect of great skiing weather. She grins, thinking of her hero, Staci Mannella, a partially sighted ski racer on the U.S. Paralympic Ski Team.

2 Evie is zooming down the powdery slopes at an incredible 40 miles an hour. While that is fast for anyone, it is absolutely astounding for a blind skier. Evie was born with cataracts, which make the lenses of her eyes hard and cloudy. She can only see light and dark shapes up close, though nothing is clear.

3 However, Evie's vision is crystal clear on one thing: her aspiration of winning a gold medal for the U.S. in the 2018 Paralympics. Today, Evie will take her time trials to see how fast she can ski the slalom course—a steep, half-mile mountain track with markers to weave around on the descent.

4 Suddenly, Evie is buffeted by a frosty, inhospitable wind, and she plants her ski poles in the snow.

5 "That wind is howling!" a female voice shouts from close behind her.

6 Evie jumps.

7 "Mom, you scared me!" Evie complains.

8 "Sorry, Evie," replies her mother. "I was certain you'd hear me ski over to you."

9 "With this wind, it's tough to hear anything."

10 Now Evie is apprehensive. Though wind doesn't bother most skiers, it adversely affects Evie's hearing, which is crucial for a blind skier. As her coach and guide, Evie's mother skis down the slalom course in front of her. Evie chases after at top speed, following the instructions her mother calls out, such as when to pivot around the markers. Skiers on the national team have special radios in their helmets so they can communicate with their guides during a run, but radio helmets are pricey.

GO ON →

11 "This wind is really powerful," says Mrs. McQueen, with palpable concern in her voice. "This is going to be a problem. Maybe I should call your father down by the finish line and tell him you'll take your time trial another day."

12 Once again, Evie thinks of her hero, Staci Mannella, one of the youngest and fastest skiers on the U.S. Team. Being nearly blind isn't a hindrance to record-breaking Staci.

13 Through skittering clouds, the sun makes an unexpected appearance, transforming the snow into a field of diamonds. Feeling the sun's comforting warmth on her cheeks, Evie's nerves are calmed and her determination is invigorated.

14 "The conditions are not great, but I think we should go for it. If my time is fast in this wind, the Paralympic team will be impressed. They'll send Staci Mannella herself to sign me up!"

15 Mrs. McQueen beams, giving Evie an encouraging hug. "Okay, Speed Queen, let's do it!"

16 Evie skis to her starting place behind her mother, and soon they are off. The wind picks up, making a slow start, but she battles to stay close to her mother. Even with the wind in her face, her goal lay closer than ever.

GO ON →

Name: _____ Date: _____

11 **Part A**

Which phrase **best** states the meaning of the word **hindrance** as it is used in paragraph 12?

(A) something that presents a hurdle

(B) something that presents a question

(C) something that presents an advantage

(D) something that presents an opportunity

Part B

Which detail from the story **best** helps the reader determine the meaning of the word **hindrance**?

(A) ". . . radio helmets are pricey." (paragraph 10)

(B) ". . . going to be a problem." (paragraph 11)

(C) ". . . transforming the snow into a field of diamonds." (paragraph 13)

(D) ". . . the Paralympic team will be impressed." (paragraph 14)

GO ON →

Copyright © McGraw-Hill Education

Grade 6 · Unit Assessment · Unit 3

97

12 **Part A**

What theme is **best** developed in the story?

(A) Even great athletes sometimes fail.

(B) The best plans sometimes have to be changed.

(C) Overcoming fear can help you achieve your goal.

(D) Success comes easily when you have someone to admire.

Part B

Which sentence from the story **best** supports the answer to Part A?

(A) "She grins, thinking of her hero, Staci Mannella, a partially sighted ski racer on the U.S. Paralympic Ski Team." (paragraph 1)

(B) "Though wind doesn't bother most skiers, it adversely affects Evie's hearing, which is crucial for a blind skier." (paragraph 10)

(C) "Feeling the sun's comforting warmth on her cheeks, Evie's nerves are calmed and her determination is invigorated." (paragraph 13)

(D) "The wind picks up, making a slow start, but she battles to stay close to her mother." (paragraph 16)

GO ON →

Read the article "The First Submarines." Then answer questions 13 and 14.

The First Submarines

1 Alexander the Great was a Greek king who ruled a large territory from the Mediterranean Sea to the Indian Ocean over 2,000 years ago. He was a great believer in new weapons that could help his army during a battle. In fact, he was likely one of the first people to use a new technology that would become one of the most feared military weapons in history: the submarine. However, when he explored the floor of the sea in a glass barrel, he saw little military use for the device. He was simply an adventurer who wanted to see more than he could view from the water's surface.

2 Alexander the Great's glass barrel submarine was lowered to the sea floor by a long chain. The connection to a boat on the surface may explain why it was not seen as a useful tool for war. Over the next 1,500 years, technological advances led to the development of many different submarines, but the wood, iron, and leather building materials used for normal boats did not hold up well under water. These first submarines could not move well and had no way of making air for the crew to breathe. Also, submarines could not be propelled by the methods used by surface boats—rowing and sailing.

3 As nations explored and settled overseas lands, naval power became more important. A large fleet of boats could transport troops, attack cities, and block supply lines. Torpedoes were invented in the 1860s to sink ships. However, they had to be launched from other surface boats. They were not effective against a well-armed navy. Military leaders needed a vessel that could quickly and quietly launch torpedoes. They increased their efforts to build a functional submarine.

4 During the American Civil War, the Confederate States Navy showed the military value of submarines by sinking thirty-four Union ships. In World War I, German submarines were feared raiders of the Atlantic Ocean. They sank many navy and merchant ships. Almost every nation involved in World War II had a fleet of submarines. By this time, the problems of power, air supply, and navigation had been solved. Submarines could travel long distances and attack without warning. Unfortunately for submarine crews, however, the radar (which uses radio waves) and sonar (which uses sound waves) used for underwater navigation also allowed surface ships to detect submarines. New defenses were made to limit the usefulness of submarines during battle. With this technology, the British were able to detect German submarines.

GO ON →

5   Today, submarines are better known for their peaceful and scientific work. A long history of exploration and scientific study with submarines stretches all the way back to Alexander the Great's glass barrel. For example, in the early 1900s, an American engineer named Simon Lake designed submarines and tested them by searching for sunken ships and gold coins on the ocean floor. Lake's submarines had larger windows, a periscope, and a special hatch for divers.

6   Submarine technology continues to improve as people set new performance goals. Nuclear power has made it possible for submarines to go faster than nearly all surface ships. They can also remain under water for months. Today, scientists are working on ways to replace gas-guzzling airplanes and cargo ships that contaminate the air and oceans. Perhaps in the future, clean-fuel-burning submarines will be the main carriers of cargo and passengers across the world's oceans.

GO ON →

13 **Part A**

What was Alexander the Great's primary purpose for using a submarine?

(A) He did it out of scientific curiosity.

(B) He did it to test out new materials.

(C) He wanted to find a navigation route for his navy.

(D) He wanted to find a new weapon to gain a military advantage.

Part B

Which sentence from the article **best** supports the answer to Part A?

(A) "He was a great believer in new weapons that could help his army during a battle." (paragraph 1)

(B) "He was simply an adventurer who wanted to see more than he could view from the water's surface." (paragraph 1)

(C) "The connection to a boat on the surface may explain why it was not seen as a useful tool for war." (paragraph 2)

(D) "These first submarines could not move well and had no way of making air for the crew to breathe." (paragraph 2)

14 What were **two** effects of the development of radar and sonar?

(A) Submarines could be invisible to enemies and attack without warning.

(B) The British were able to protect themselves from German submarines.

(C) Torpedoes could be launched from underwater rather than from surface boats.

(D) They allowed people to breathe underwater.

(E) Submarines could travel faster than nearly all surface ships.

(F) Submarines became less effective as war ships.

GO ON →

Refer to the story "Blind Racer" and the article "The First Submarines." Then answer question 15.

15 Both "Blind Racer" and "The First Submarines" discuss challenges that stand in the way of accomplishing goals. Describe these challenges and how they are overcome. Use details from both texts to support your answer.

_____

_____

_____

_____

_____

_____

_____

_____

_____

_____

_____

_____

_____

GO ON →

The following passage needs revision. Read the passage. Then answer questions 16 through 25.

Few people would ever guess that Steven Spielberg __(1)__ the target of bullies. But the director of popular movies such as *E.T. the Extra-Terrestrial* and *Indiana Jones* __(2)__ from bullying as a child.

Born in 1946 in Cincinnati, Steven __(3)__ making movies at home with his dad's camera and with the help of his younger sisters, Sue, Anne, and Nancy. He __(4)__ confident as he got older. But one day at school, a bully __(5)__ Steven and pushed him into the water fountain. Steven then asked __(6)__ to be the hero of his next movie, *Escape to Nowhere*. Surprisingly, the boy agreed. Steven __(7)__ the bully on his own terms.

Since then, Steven Spielberg has made many films. In 1993, he __(8)__ for a film called *Schindler's List*. It told how Oskar Schindler saved more than 1,200 Jews during World War II. Spielberg __(9)__ an Oscar for Best Director for that film. In 1998, Spielberg received another Oscar for *Saving Private Ryan*, which was also about World War II.

Today, Steven Spielberg __(10)__ movies and works with a number of organizations.

GO ON →

16 Which answer should go in blank (1)?

(A) are

(B) being

(C) was

17 Which answer should go in blank (2)?

(A) did suffer

(B) can suffer

(C) may suffer

18 Which answer should go in blank (3)?

(A) enjoy

(B) enjoyed

(C) enjoying

19 Which answer should go in blank (4)?

(A) grew

(B) grows

(C) is growing

20 Which answer should go in blank (5)?

(A) taunts

(B) taunted

(C) is taunting

GO ON →

21 Which answer should go in blank (6)?

- (A) loudly
- (B) invited
- (C) the boy

22 Which answer should go in blank (7)?

- (A) beating
- (B) had beaten
- (C) was beaten

23 Which answer should go in blank (8)?

- (A) is recognized
- (B) was recognized
- (C) have recognized

24 Which answer should go in blank (9)?

- (A) win
- (B) winned
- (C) won

25 Which answer should go in blank (10)?

- (A) produce
- (B) produces
- (C) producing

STOP

Literary Analysis Task

Today you will read the story "A Sudden Turn" and the poem "The Snowstorm." As you read these texts, pay attention to the themes and topics in each text to help prepare you to write an essay.

Read the story "A Sudden Turn." Then answer questions 1 through 3.

A Sudden Turn

1   During the last week of summer vacation, Gabe woke in a shaft of sunshine shimmering through the window. He blinked, holding an arm up against the glare. Sitting up, he swung his legs off the bed, wondering what his family would end up doing today. Their month at the shore house had shrunk to its final days, and Gabe wanted to make each one count. Okay, so the house wasn't technically *on* the shore, but the ocean was only about a five-minute drive away.

2   Gabe rose and strode to the open window, where a couple of flies buzzed against the screen. Starlings flitted and *cheeped* in the big oak tree before taking to the sky in a big, leaf-ruffling *whoosh*. Gabe watched them swoop into the blue, marveling at the rich color that stretched in all directions, unmarred by even the smallest, white chalk-scratch of a cloud. There was a name for that shade of blue, *azure* or *indigo*—whatever, he'd look it up later. Because it would be a shame to waste this kind of a day by looking at it. Gabe pulled on shorts and a T-shirt and galloped down the stairs.

3   In the kitchen, his mom was lining cereal boxes up on the table, while his dad fussed over the coffee pot. His eight-year-old brother Eli looked groggy, staring with half-lidded eyes at his empty bowl. The radio blared in the background, the newsperson's excited voice speeding away, an unwelcome reminder of everyday city life.

4   "Can we turn this off?" asked Gabe, walking toward the radio.

5   "Leave it on—we're listening to the weather report," said his dad.

6   "If you're curious about the weather, look outside," said Gabe, pointing to the window.

7   "Yeah, I know," said his dad, pouring coffee into two mugs and setting them on the table. "But apparently, that hurricane—Brad, I think they're calling it, the one they thought was going to hit farther north—well, they think it might have taken a sharp turn. Which means we need to be on the lookout."

GO ON →

8 Gabe rolled his eyes as he headed for the refrigerator. Everyone liked to get all worked up about the weather any time there was the slightest hint of a storm. Gabe remembered taping big X's on the windows one year, and stocking up on flashlight batteries and candles. But nothing ever happened, and one look at the sky told him that today would be just fine, too.

9 After breakfast, Gabe helped his mom do the dishes while Eli and his dad started making sandwiches for the beach. But his parents insisted that the decision to go on an outing wasn't official yet, and as his mom kept flashing anxious looks out the window, Gabe wondered if maybe he should start worrying, too.

10 And then the winds started picking up. It began as a refreshing breeze, gently wafting the kitchen curtains, but soon surged into gusts that flung dirt through the screens. The back door slammed, and suddenly, the room was cast in shadow, like someone had turned out the lights. Gabe and Eli stepped out onto the back porch and watched clouds gather, billowing in dark shades of iron, slate, and smoke. The wind twisted the trees, snatching away small twigs and tearing off leaves.

11 "Whoa—it was a beach day a minute ago," said Eli, and Gabe understood his amazement at the sudden turn. Less than an hour ago, he had woken to a tranquil, unmoving, and infinite blue. Now, he was watching the sturdy old oak bend and sway, bowing to the garage as if paying homage to an emperor.

12 "That branch is looking awfully flimsy," said his mom, who had joined them on the porch.

13 "It's going to take more than a strong wind to take that down—I mean, look how thick it is," said his dad. His parents discussed moving the car out of the garage, but when the wind started hurling gravel at the back door, decided to leave it be.

14 Over the next few hours, they all huddled in the living room, which had the fewest windows. When the rains had come, they'd shut all the windows, then drawn the curtains, making the house even darker. They'd turned on the lights, then when the electricity went out, lit candles in glass lanterns. The wind was a wild thing, howling and shrieking and demanding to be let in. Doing their best to ignore it, they spread a quilt on the floor and ate their beach picnic, and at some point, Gabe dozed off.

15 When he woke up, it was still raining, but the worst of it had passed. The winds had died down a bit, and soon they seemed unremarkable. The clouds had brightened, and someone had opened the curtains to let in the daylight. Hearing a shout, Gabe hurried to the kitchen, where the rest of the family was standing at the screen door.

GO ON →

16 "I guess Brad was stronger than the oak tree," his dad sighed. A branch as thick as a man had fallen, smashing the garage—and presumably, the car.

17 Gabe shook his head in awe, thinking about what he had witnessed today, and wondering what he would discover when he finally ventured out beyond the house toward the shore.

GO ON →

1 **Part A**

What does the word **tranquil** mean as it is used in paragraph 11 of "A Sudden Turn"?

(A) calm

(B) brilliant

(C) surprising

(D) predictable

Part B

Which word from paragraph 11 is the **best** clue to the meaning of **tranquil** in Part A?

(A) beach

(B) sudden

(C) unmoving

(D) sturdy

GO ON →

2 **Part A**

In "A Sudden Turn," how does Gabe's attitude about the weather change during the story?

(A) from annoyed to excited

(B) from nervous to frightened

(C) from delighted to distressed

(D) from unworried to astonished

Part B

Which **two** sentences from the story **best** support the answer to Part A?

(A) "Their month at the shore house had shrunk to its final days, and Gabe wanted to make each one count." (paragraph 1)

(B) "Gabe rose and strode to the open window, where a couple of flies buzzed against the screen." (paragraph 2)

(C) "Because it would be a shame to waste this kind of a day by looking at it." (paragraph 2)

(D) "But nothing ever happened, and one look at the sky told him that today would be just fine, too." (paragraph 8)

(E) "Doing their best to ignore it, they spread a quilt on the floor and ate their beach picnic, and at some point, Gabe dozed off." (paragraph 14)

(F) "Gabe shook his head in awe, thinking about what he had witnessed today, and wondering what he would discover when he finally ventured out beyond the house toward the shore." (paragraph 17)

GO ON →

Name: _____ Date: _____

3 For the story "A Sudden Turn," use the story map to create a summary by writing the correct details from the list in the correct boxes.

Main Character: Gabe	Setting: Shore house
Conflict:	
Event 1:	
Event 2:	
Event 3:	
Resolution:	

Details

Gabe argues with his parents about the radio.

Gabe hears that Hurricane Brad may be heading their way.

Gabe appreciates the weather's powerful, unpredictable nature.

Gabe is upset that summer vacation is ending.

Gabe refuses to believe that a hurricane is approaching.

Gabe sees the garage crushed by a downed oak branch.

Gabe wakes to a beautiful, sunny day.

Gabe announces that he wants to go to the beach.

GO ON →

Read the poem "The Snowstorm." Then answer questions 4 and 5.

The Snowstorm

by Ralph Waldo Emerson

Announced by all the trumpets of the sky,
Arrives the snow, and, driving o'er the fields,
Seems nowhere to alight[1]: the whited air
Hides hills and woods, the river, and the heaven,
5   And veils the farmhouse at the garden's end.
The sled and traveler stopped, the courier's feet
Delayed, all friends shut out, the housemates sit
Around the radiant fireplace, enclosed
In a tumultuous privacy of storm.

10 Come see the north wind's masonry[2].
Out of an unseen quarry evermore
Furnished with tile, the fierce artificer[3]
Curves his white bastions with projected roof
Round every wayward stake, or tree, or door.
15 Speeding, the myriad-handed[4], his wild work
So fanciful, so savage, nought cares he
For number or proportion. Mockingly,
On coop or kennel he hangs Parian[5] wreaths;
A swan-like form invests the hidden thorn;
20 Fills up the farmer's lane from wall to wall,
Maugre the farmer sighs; and, at the gate,
A tapering turret overtops the work.
And when his hours are numbered, and the world
Is all his own, retiring, as he were not,
25 Leaves, when the sun appears, astonished Art[6]
To mimic in slow structures, stone by stone,
Built in an age, the mad wind's night-work,
The frolic architecture of snow.

---

[1] alight—come to a rest
[2] masonry—stonework
[3] artificer—skilled artist or craftsman
[4] myriad-handed—many-handed
[5] Parian—a type of fine-grained white marble. Taken from quarries on the Greek island of Paros in the
   Aegean Sea, it was used by ancient Greek sculptors in many famous works.
[6] Art—artists

GO ON →

4 **Part A**

Read lines 26 and 27 from "The Snowstorm."

> To mimic in slow structures, stone by stone,
> Built in an age, the mad wind's night-work,

Which sentence **best** states the meaning of these lines?

(A) A sculptor uses stone to make long-lasting works of art.

(B) What the storm creates in one night takes an artist years.

(C) While snow may be wildly beautiful, art takes planning.

(D) Artists often try to capture the beauty of a snowstorm.

Part B

Which detail from the poem suggests the same idea as the answer to Part A?

(A) ". . . the whited air / Hides hills and woods . . ." (lines 3 and 4)

(B) ". . . the housemates sit / Around the radiant fireplace . . ." (lines 7 and 8)

(C) "Speeding, the myriad-handed, his wild work / So fanciful . . ." (lines 15 and 16)

(D) "And when his hours are numbered, and the world / Is all his own . . ." (lines 23 and 24)

GO ON →

5 **Part A**

Read line 10 from "The Snowstorm."

> Come see the north wind's masonry.

How does this line contribute to the overall structure of the poem?

(A) It suggests that snow can be as beautiful as a painting.

(B) It demonstrates the destructive power of a snowstorm.

(C) It establishes a comparison between the snowstorm and a sculptor.

(D) It introduces the idea that snow can be used to make actual structures.

Part B

Which detail from the poem **best** supports the answer to Part A?

(A) "Announced by all the trumpets of the sky, / Arrives the snow ..."
(lines 1 and 2)

(B) "And veils the farmhouse at the garden's end." (line 5)

(C) "... the fierce artificer / Curves his white bastions with projected roof"
(lines 12 and 13)

(D) "... nought cares he / For number or proportion...." (lines 16 and 17)

GO ON →

Name: _____ Date: _____

Refer to the story "A Sudden Turn" and the poem "The Snowstorm." Then answer questions 6 and 7.

6 Read the central ideas in the list and decide whether they are found in the story "A Sudden Turn," the poem "The Snowstorm," or in both. Write **each** idea in the correct location in the chart.

"A Sudden Turn"	Both	"The Snowstorm"

Central Ideas

People can be inspired by nature to create beautiful works.
People often underestimate the power of nature.
Nature can be unpredictable.
Nature can fill people with both fear and wonder.

7 You have read the story "A Sudden Turn" and the poem "The Snowstorm." Write an essay that identifies a theme common to both texts and compares and contrasts the methods each text uses to develop this theme. Be sure to support your response with evidence from **both** texts.

Write your essay on a separate sheet of paper.

STOP

Question	Correct Answer	Content Focus	CCSS	Complexity
1	see below	Prefixes and Suffixes	RL.6.1, RL.6.4, L.6.4b	DOK 1
2A	D	Synonyms and Antonyms	RL.6.1, RL.6.4, L.6.5b	DOK 2
2B	A	Synonyms and Antonyms	RL.6.1, RL.6.4, L.6.5b	DOK 2
3	B, F	Third-Person Limited Point of View	RL.6.1, RL.6.6	DOK 2
4A	C	Theme	RL.6.1, RL.6.2	DOK 3
4B	C	Theme	RL.6.1, RL.6.2	DOK 2
5A	B	Theme	RL.6.1, RL.6.2	DOK 3
5B	D	Theme	RL.6.1, RL.6.2	DOK 2
6A	C, E	Synonyms and Antonyms	RI.6.1, RI.6.4, L.6.5b	DOK 2
6B	A	Synonyms and Antonyms	RI.6.1, RI.6.4, L.6.5b	DOK 2
7	see below	Prefixes and Suffixes	RI.6.1, RI.6.4, L.6.4b	DOK 1
8	see below	Text Structure: Cause and Effect	RI.6.1, RI.6.3	DOK 2
9A	D	Main Idea and Key Details	RI.1.1, RI.6.2	DOK 3
9B	C	Main Idea and Key Details	RI.6.1, RI.6.2	DOK 2
10	see below	Text Structure: Sequence	RI.6.1, RI.6.5	DOK 3
11A	A	Context Clues: Paragraph Clues	RL.6.1, RL.6.4, L.6.4a	DOK 2
11B	B	Context Clues: Paragraph Clues	RL.6.1, RL.6.4, L.6.4a	DOK 2
12A	C	Theme	RL.6.1, RL.6.2	DOK 3
12B	C	Theme	RL.6.1, RL.6.2	DOK 2
13A	A	Main Idea and Key Details	RI.6.1, RI.6.2	DOK 2
13B	B	Main Idea and Key Details	RI.6.1, RI.6.2	DOK 2
14	B, F	Text Structure: Cause and Effect	RI.6.1, RI.6.3	DOK 2
15	see below	Compare Across Texts	W.6.9	DOK 4
16	C	Linking Verbs	L.6.1	DOK 1
17	A	Main and Helping Verbs	L.6.1	DOK 1

Question	Correct Answer	Content Focus	CCSS	Complexity
18	B	Simple Tenses	L.6.1	DOK 1
19	A	Simple Tenses	L.6.1	DOK 1
20	B	Action Verbs; Direct and Indirect Objects	L.6.1	DOK 1
21	C	Action Verbs; Direct and Indirect Objects	L.6.1	DOK 1
22	B	Irregular Verbs	L.6.1	DOK 1
23	B	Main and Helping Verbs	L.6.1	DOK 1
24	C	Irregular Verbs	L.6.1	DOK 1
25	B	Simple Tenses	L.6.1	DOK 1

Comprehension: Selected Response 3, 4A, 4B, 5A, 5B, 8, 9A, 9B, 12A, 12B, 13A, 13B, 14	/16	%
Comprehension: Constructed Response 10, 15	/6	%
Vocabulary 1, 2A, 2B, 6A, 6B, 7, 11A, 11B	/10	%
English Language Conventions 16–25	/10	%
Total Unit Assessment Score	/42	%

1 Students should write the following meanings:
- unusual: not familiar
- intensity: state of determination

7 Students should write the following meanings:
- ferocity: a violent quality
- thankful: filled with appreciation
- regained: something gotten again

8 Students should draw lines to match the following causes and effects:
- Effect: "Shackleton ordered his crew to prepare for a long wait."
  —Cause:　(1) "The *Endurance* got stuck in a field of ice.
- Effect: "The objective of the Shackleton expedition changed to survival."
  —Causes:　(1) "Supplies, such as fuel for fires, were low."
  　　　　　(2) "The ship was trapped a long distance away from the planned landing point."
  　　　　　(3) "Ice broke through the walls of the *Endurance*."

10 **2-point response:** The author organizes the article using a sequential structure so that readers can better follow Shackleton's expedition. Readers learn that Shackleton and his crew got stuck "less than two months into their journey." The author then explains that the ship sank "11 months after it was first trapped in the ice," which helps readers understand how long they had to struggle on the ice.

Name: _____

15 **4-point response:** In "Blind Racer," Evie's biggest challenge is her sight. She also had to face high winds and a lack of equipment. Evie overcame these challenges by focusing on her goal and thinking of her hero, Staci Mannella. Staci is another nearly blind skier who has won many awards for the U.S. Paralympic team. Evie chose to do her time trial because she knew Staci would not quit. Her mother had to shout extra loud, and Evie needed to concentrate and follow her very closely. This is how Evie overcame the challenges she faced to work toward her goal.

In "The First Submarines," the basic challenges were how to make a submarine that could move around underwater and create its own air. In some ways, the problem of moving around underwater was similar to the problem that Evie faced. Underwater, it's hard to see, but you have to know when to turn and avoid obstacles. Submarines use radar and sonar for this, instead of a guide. People then improved submarines further for different reasons. Some wanted to use them as military weapons, so they added nuclear power for speed. Others wanted to explore the ocean for science or adventure, so scientists created big windows and diving hatches.

Answer Key

Name: _____

Question	Answer	CCSS	Complexity
1A	A	RL.6.1, RL.6.4, L.6.4a	DOK 2
1B	C		DOK 2
2A	D	RL.6.1, RL.6.3	DOK 3
2B	D, F		DOK 2
3	see below	RL.6.1, RL.6.2, RL.6.3	DOK 3
4A	B	RL.6.1, RL.6.4, L.6.5a	DOK 2
4B	C		DOK 2
5A	C	RL.6.1, RL.6.5	DOK 3
5B	C		DOK 2
6	see below	RL.6.1, RL.6.2, RL.6.9	DOK 3
7	see below	RL.6.1, RL.6.9 W.6.1, W.6.2, W.6.4–W.6.10 L.6.1, L.6.2, L.6.3, L.6.6	DOK 4

Comprehension 2A, 2B, 3, 5A, 5B, 6		/8	%
Vocabulary 1A, 1B, 4A, 4B		/4	%
Prose Constructed Response 7		/4 [RC] /12 [WE] /3 [LC]	%
Total Literary Analysis Score		/31	%

5 Students should write the following details in the chart:
- Conflict: Gabe refuses to believe that a hurricane is approaching.
- Event 1: Gabe wakes to a beautiful, sunny day.
- Event 2: Gabe hears that Hurricane Brad may be heading their way.
- Event 3: Gabe sees the garage crushed by a downed oak branch.
- Resolution: Gabe appreciates the weather's powerful, unpredictable nature.

6 Students should write the central ideas in the chart as follows:
- "A Sudden Turn"—"People often underestimate the power of Nature," "Nature can be unpredictable."
- Both—"Nature can fill people with both fear and wonder."
- "The Snowstorm"—"People can be inspired by nature to create beautiful works."

7 **19-point anchor paper:**

Although the story centers on a hurricane and the poem on a snowstorm, both texts focus on nature. Each text explores several ideas about nature, but one theme common to both deals with respecting or appreciating the two sides of nature. In other words, "People who understand nature view it with both fear and wonder.

In "A Sudden Turn," Gabe begins his day by going to the window and admiring a beautiful summer day—one of the last of his vacation. In paragraph 2, he first watches birds in a tree: "Starlings flitted and cheeped in the big oak tree before taking to the sky in a big, leaf-ruffling whoosh." Then his gaze follows them into the sky: "Gabe watched them swoop into the blue, marveling at the rich color that stretched in all directions, unmarred by even the smallest, white chalk-scratch of a cloud." After trying to figure out the exact name for this particular blue, he decides to join his family for breakfast. So the first two paragraphs with their descriptions of nature's beauty, and Gabe's response to it, convey the idea that he, like most people, admires this side of nature.

When his parents tell him that a hurricane may be headed their way, Gabe refuses to believe that it's possible. And in paragraph 8, he remembers a time when his family prepared for a hurricane that never came. "But nothing ever happened, and one look at the sky told him that today would be just fine, too." Here, Gabe doesn't to truly appreciate, or understand, nature. His parents express this, too. In paragraphs 12–13, they find it hard to believe that a strong wind could take down a sturdy oak branch. The hurricane really hits in paragraph 14, where the author describes the wind as "a wild thing, howling and shrieking and demanding to be let in." And as the hurricane moves on, Gabe shakes his head "in awe, thinking about what he had witnessed today, and wondering what he would discover when he finally ventured out beyond the house toward the shore." In this way, the story conveys Gabe's new respect for nature. He has learned to appreciate everything it can do.

"The Snowstorm" expresses a similar theme. The two-verse structure of the poem itself provides a way to portray nature's dual nature. The first stanza describes the snowstorm moving in, bringing all normal activities to a halt. "The sled and traveler stopped, the courier's feet / Delayed, all friends shut out, the housemates sit / Around the radiant fireplace . . ." This image echoes the scene in "A Sudden Turn," in which Gabe's family hunkers down in the living room, eating an indoor picnic by candlelight. So the poem's first stanza conveys one idea about respecting nature: fearing its power enough to stay inside and out of its way.

The second stanza, however, illustrates a different picture. Here, the poet leaves the people sitting around their fireplace and focuses solely on the beautiful forms created by the snow. "Come see the north wind's masonry," reads line 10, comparing shapes made by the snow to sculptures made from stone provided by "an unseen quarry evermore / Furnished with tile." (lines 11–12) Nature itself is named "the fierce artificer," who carves "tapering turrets" and "white bastions." This "frolic architecture of snow" is portrayed with a sense of awe, adding a sense of wonder to the fearful respect for nature illustrated in the first half of the poem.

Read the play "The Beech Tree." Then answer questions 1 through 5.

The Beech Tree

Act I

A summer afternoon in Lyndonville. An enormous, leafy tree fills CENTER STAGE. It is so huge that only the lower part of the trunk is visible. Two massive lower limbs extend out of sight at STAGE LEFT and STAGE RIGHT. From the middle of the left limb, EMILY, a 7-year-old girl, swings on a simple rope swing. On the right limb, OWEN, an 11-year-old boy, plays and climbs. In front of the tree trunk, MOTHER and FATHER sit opposite each other at a table. FATHER is reading a newspaper. MOTHER is typing on a laptop computer.

NEIGHBOR 1 shuffles into sight from STAGE RIGHT. He pauses, facing the family.

NEIGHBOR 1: You Andersons certainly look cool on this steamy afternoon!

FATHER: (*looking up from his paper*) Yes, thanks to our beech tree!

MOTHER: (*smiling up from her laptop*) We try not to take her for granted!

EMILY: She has the best kind of arms for holding up swings!

OWEN: Someday I'm going to build a tree house up here and live in it!

NEIGHBOR 1: Well, what an idea. Good luck with it, and good afternoon!

FATHER and MOTHER: (*together*) Have a nice day.

NEIGHBOR 1 shuffles past and exits STAGE LEFT. All go back to what they were doing. LIGHTS FADE.

GO ON →

Act II

Scene 1

Three months later: the same place, on a dark and stormy autumn night. Frequent flashes of lightning reveal the tree trunk and branches, which are now mostly bare. Dry leaves fall from tree limbs out of sight above and swirl about the stage. Rumbles and cracks of thunder follow each lightning flash. Suddenly, a colossal lightning bolt strikes the tree. With a tremendous crash, the tree's massive limbs fall to the stage. The lightning flickers several more times, lighting up what is left of the tree. The tall trunk remains standing, though the top has fallen off and the two side limbs have each broken off a few feet from the trunk. The lightning flashes and rumbles of thunder become fewer and weaker, suggesting that the storm is passing. DARKNESS.

Scene 2

Early the next morning: the same place. MOTHER, EMILY, and OWEN stand near the tree. NEIGHBORS 1, 2, and 3 enter slowly from STAGE RIGHT and STAGE LEFT. They gather to stare at the wreckage of the tree. At first they are too stunned to speak. Then NEIGHBOR 1 breaks the silence.

NEIGHBOR 1: What a sad sight! I can hardly bear to look at it. That tree has stood there as long as I can remember!

NEIGHBOR 2: My grandparents said it was already huge when they were born!

NEIGHBOR 3: In the old days, the town used to hold Fourth of July picnics under it. I have pictures taken at this spot in 1889. All the women wore white linen dresses, and the men wore white jackets, ties, and hats. They all sat here, enjoying the shade.

MOTHER: That was before our house was built.

OWEN: Now I won't get to build my tree house after all!

EMILY: Does this mean the rest of our tree has to be cut down?

Enter FATHER, STAGE LEFT. In one hand he is carrying a chainsaw. As everyone on stage looks on, he walks toward the tree and stops to look at it. After a few moments, he gives the chainsaw cord a sharp tug, and the engine roars. Raising the saw with both hands, he steps toward the tree. LIGHTS FADE OUT.

GO ON →

Act III

Thirty years later: a summer afternoon, the same place. The house is gone. Where the beech tree stood there is now a large, roughly carved wooden sculpture that resembles both the wrecked tree after the storm and also a human figure with arms outstretched. Nearby is a marker with text printed on it. Enter EMILY and OWEN, now adults.

EMILY: Do you remember my swing?

OWEN: Of course. I can still see you flying back and forth on it. You never gave me a turn!

EMILY: (*smiling*) You had other things on your mind.

OWEN: I was imagining the tree house I would build!

EMILY: And you became an artist, just like Dad. The apple doesn't fall far from the tree!

OWEN: At least his masterpiece is still here.

EMILY: (*reading the sign aloud*) "'Welcome,' chainsaw art by Alex Anderson, 2011. A European beech tree once stood here. When it was struck by lightning in 2011, it stood 137 feet tall, with a diameter of 10 feet, and its age was estimated at 185 years. As a modern sculpture, what is left of the tree is now a popular landmark. People come from miles around to stand where you are standing now. Welcome to Lyndonville!"

EMILY and OWEN remain gazing at the sculpture as LIGHTS FADE.

GO ON →

1 Circle **two** words from the play that are homophones.

scene	bear
looks	huge
bare	act
colossal	saw

2 **Part A**

Read the sentence from the play.

> *Then NEIGHBOR 1 breaks the silence.*

What does the phrase **breaks the silence** mean?

(A) speaks first

(B) looks quietly

(C) gets angry

(D) feels sadness

Part B

Which sentence from the play **best** helps the reader understand the answer to Part A?

(A) *"They gather to stare at the wreckage of the tree."*

(B) *"At first they are too stunned to speak."*

(C) *"'That tree has stood there as long as I can remember!'"*

(D) *"'Now I won't get to build my tree house after all!'"*

GO ON →

3 **Part A**

Which statement **best** expresses a theme developed in the play?

(A) Nothing good lasts forever.

(B) Change makes people stronger.

(C) Protecting the environment is critical.

(D) Positive things can come from a bad situation.

Part B

Which detail from the play **best** supports the answer to Part A?

(A) Owen became an artist just like his dad.

(B) People enjoyed the shade of the tree in the old days.

(C) Emily and Owen's father turns the tree into a sculpture.

(D) The neighbors remember how long the tree has been there.

4 Select **two** sentences from the play that **best** support the theme.

(A) "'She has the best kind of arms for holding up swings!'"

(B) *"The tall trunk remains standing, though the top has fallen off and the two side limbs have each broken off a few feet from the trunk."*

(C) "'My grandparents said it was already huge when they were born!'"

(D) *"Where the beech tree stood there is now a large, roughly carved wooden sculpture that resembles both the wrecked tree after the storm and also a human figure with arms outstretched."*

(E) "'When it was struck by lightning in 2011, it stood 137 feet tall, with a diameter of 10 feet, and its age was estimated at 185 years.'"

(F) "'People come from miles around to stand where you are standing now.'"

GO ON →

5 How does Emily and Owen's attitude toward the beech tree change from the beginning to the end of the play? Mark the boxes below to complete each sentence.

In the beginning, Emily and Owen view the tree as _____.

	a window into the 1800s
	something they can play with
	a place in which they can sit and relax
	something to protect them from the hot sun

At the end, they view it as _____.

	a reminder of how cruel nature can be
	a symbol of the storm that destroyed it
	a piece of artwork that reminds them of their childhood
	a tourist attraction that does not mean much to them anymore

GO ON →

Read the article "Margaret Mee, Botanical Artist." Then answer questions 6 through 10.

Margaret Mee, Botanical Artist

1   On the Internet, you can find three particular video clips filmed in May 1988 about a special woman. The first is called "The Search." It opens with images of a slight, 78-year-old English woman leaning from the railing of a Brazilian riverboat. The boat is traveling up the Rio Negro, a river whose dark, tea-colored waters flow into the great, muddy Amazon.

2   In the next scene, the boat has pulled up to a riverbank. The lady has spied a certain kind of cactus growing on the bark of a nearby tree and is standing on the boat's rooftop to examine it. As she gets closer and closer to the specimen, she remarks about how marvelous it is to see the beautiful plant. She notices that it has thorns and that the leaves change from green to red when they are exposed to the sun. Sticking out from the side of the cactus are two buds. One is almost ready to open.

Looking for Moonflowers

3   The woman in the film clips is Margaret Mee. Born in England in 1909, she moved to Brazil in 1952. Beginning at age 47, she made 15 long river trips—some lasting months—into the Amazon rainforest to document its flowering plants. She braved all sorts of tropical perils, from malaria to scorpions, poisonous animals, and even a few unsavory people. None of them stopped her.

4   Margaret knew that many of the plant species of the Amazon region had never been recorded before. She accurately predicted that some would soon become extinct. Much to her dismay, expansive areas of the rainforest were being logged and burned to make way for roads and ranches. She made it her job to preserve the plants of Amazonia for future people—by drawing, painting, and describing them.

5   Margaret's expedition of 1988 had a particular botanical subject: *Selenicereus wittii*, the "moonflower cactus." It was named after Selene, the ancient Greek goddess of the moon. For years, Margaret's greatest ambition had been to paint the life cycle of this plant's night-blooming flower.

6   On two previous journeys up the Rio Negro, she had found the plant but not its flowers. The cactus is so rare that no one had ever been able to record its blooming in nature. It blooms in moonlight, only long enough to attract insects to its pollen. The flower opens when the sun sets, closes when the sun rises, then dies.

GO ON →

Painting the Flowers

7 The second video clip, called "The Sketching," begins a day or two after the first. Dusk has come, and the rainforest throbs with the sounds of tropical frogs and insects. In near darkness, Margaret is now sitting in a chair on the rooftop of the riverboat. On her lap is a sketchbook, and in her hand is a pencil. While someone holds a dim, battery-powered light near her paper, she is carefully observing and expertly drawing the flower buds of the cactus she was earlier examining. From where she sits, about 10 feet above the river, the buds are slightly higher than eye level.

8 As she watches, the moonflower begins to move. As her pencil moves across the paper, a long, thin, pale petal of one bud twitches open. One by one, the flower's many petals begin to unfold.

9 The last video clip, "The Painting," shows the riverboat still pulled up to the riverbank. The morning sun is bright, and Margaret remains sitting in the rooftop chair. She has been working all night. The air appears to be warm and humid, but she seems not to care. For shade she is wearing a wide-brimmed straw hat. Her sketchbook is still on her lap, although now she is using a paintbrush and a small set of paints. She is adding the colors that couldn't be seen in the dark.

The Final Expedition

10 Unknown to Margaret Mee, the expedition of May 1988 was to be her last. Seven months later, she died in a car accident in England. What she left behind were nearly 400 botanical paintings of rare plants of Amazonia, along with many sketches and diaries of her findings in Brazil. People can see them in books or at the Royal Botanic Gardens at Kew, near London.

11 Because of the continuing changes to the Amazon rainforest, some of the plant species that inspired Margaret Mee can no longer be found. However, thanks to her work, present and future generations can learn where and how those plants grew. They can imagine how hundreds of surviving plants still grow. And they can see how the flower of one rare cactus blooms and dies in the tropical moonlight.

GO ON →

6 **Part A**

What is the meaning of **perils** as it is used in paragraph 3?

(A) dangers

(B) diseases

(C) criminals

(D) surprises

Part B

Which **three** words from paragraph 3 **best** support the answer to Part A?

(A) rainforest

(B) document

(C) braved

(D) tropical

(E) poisonous

(F) unsavory

(G) stopped

GO ON →

7 Part A

Read the sentence from paragraph 6.

> The cactus is so rare that no one had ever been able to record its blooming in nature.

What is the meaning of the word **record** as it is used in the sentence?

(A) a disk containing audio

(B) a remarkable performance

(C) state or express officially

(D) set down in writing or images

Part B

Which detail from the article **best** helps the reader determine the meaning of the word **record**?

(A) ". . . some would soon become extinct." (paragraph 4)

(B) ". . . by drawing, painting, and describing them." (paragraph 4)

(C) ". . . had a particular botanical subject . . ." (paragraph 5)

(D) ". . . only long enough to attract insects to its pollen." (paragraph 6)

GO ON →

8 **Part A**

What do paragraphs 1 and 2 show about the author's point of view?

(A) The author relates to Margaret Mee's purpose.

(B) The author wants to travel to the same places as Margaret Mee.

(C) The author recognizes Margaret Mee's deep appreciation of nature.

(D) The author thinks that Margaret Mee inspired other botanical artists.

Part B

Which detail from the article **best** supports the answer to Part A?

(A) ". . . a slight, 78-year-old English woman leaning from the railing . . ." (paragraph 1)

(B) "The boat is traveling up the Rio Negro, a river whose dark, tea-colored waters flow . . ." (paragraph 1)

(C) "The lady has spied a certain kind of cactus growing on the bark of a nearby tree . . ." (paragraph 2)

(D) ". . . she remarks about how marvelous it is to see the beautiful plant." (paragraph 2)

9 The author admires Margaret Mee's determination to capture the moonflower in bloom. Underline **two** sentences in paragraph 9 that **best** support this statement.

> 9 The last video clip, "The Painting," shows the riverboat still pulled up to the riverbank. The morning sun is bright, and Margaret remains sitting in the rooftop chair. She has been working all night. The air appears to be warm and humid, but she seems not to care. For shade she is wearing a wide-brimmed straw hat. Her sketchbook is still on her lap, although now she is using a paintbrush and a small set of paints. She is adding the colors that couldn't be seen in the dark.

GO ON →

10 **Part A**

Which statement **best** describes how the author feels about Margaret Mee's work as a botanical artist?

Ⓐ It was time-consuming.

Ⓑ It involved many frustrations.

Ⓒ It was important to understanding the rainforest.

Ⓓ It deserved celebration from the artistic community.

Part B

Which sentence from the article **best** supports the answer to Part A?

Ⓐ "Beginning at age 47, she made 15 long river trips—some lasting months—into the Amazon rainforest to document its flowering plants." (paragraph 3)

Ⓑ "On two previous journeys up the Rio Negro, she had found the plant but not its flowers." (paragraph 6)

Ⓒ "While someone holds a dim, battery-powered light near her paper, she is carefully observing and expertly drawing the flower buds of the cactus she was earlier examining." (paragraph 7)

Ⓓ "However, thanks to her work, present and future generations can learn where and how those plants grew." (paragraph 11)

GO ON →

Today you will read an article and a story about solving problems.

Read the article "Apollo 13: A Galactic Challenge." Then answer questions 11 and 12.

Apollo 13: A Galactic Challenge

1   On the heels of the successful Apollo 11 and 12 missions, NASA prepared for another Apollo mission to launch on April 11, 1970. The mission was launched under the leadership of Commander Jim Lovell and crew members Jack Swigert and Fred Haise. The three men were two days into their mission and around 200,000 miles from Earth when an oxygen tank exploded on their service module. They were only ten hours from the moon, but they would not be able to walk on the surface. The crew, together with NASA engineers back on Earth, would need every bit of skill, creativity, and training to bring the astronauts home safely.

2   The explosion caused many problems on the Apollo 13 spacecraft. The service module, the spaceship's "living room," lost power. Several critical systems, including life support and communications, were damaged. The astronauts had no choice but to shut down the main part of the spacecraft and lock themselves in the lunar lander. The small lander, intended to be used during moon exploration, was now their "lifeboat."

3   Even though this catastrophic event was considered very unlikely, the astronauts had prepared for it back on Earth. NASA training was famously thorough. Before a mission, astronauts practiced their response to many problems that never actually took place. Unfortunately, even the most careful planning had not prepared the crew for a long flight back to Earth in the lunar lander. The lander was very small. It was designed for two men to stay on the surface of the moon for only a day. It was not made for three men to live in for four days. Limited power forced them to turn off most of their equipment, including the heater. For most of the journey back to Earth, the temperature inside the lander was around 40 degrees Fahrenheit—just above freezing.

4   Soon, Commander Lovell reported that another warning light was flashing. Carbon dioxide levels in the lander were getting dangerously high; too much of the gas can cause sickness or death. People exhale carbon dioxide when they breathe, and the three astronauts were producing more carbon dioxide than the small lander could handle. The carbon dioxide removal system on the lander was too small, so they had to somehow connect it to the larger system on the main, damaged ship. A group of engineers back on Earth worked frantically to devise some kind of connecting system.

GO ON →

5 Meanwhile, the crew on the spaceship was getting dizzy and disoriented from all the carbon dioxide in their tiny lifeboat. They were only halfway back from the moon and had only a few hours of breathable air left. Finally, the engineers on Earth radioed instructions for building "the Mailbox." It was their term for a device made out of spare parts: an empty box, a breathing tube from a space suit, and even duct tape! The air finally cleared, and the crew of Apollo 13 returned safely to Earth on April 17, after four days of constant stress and danger.

6 The Apollo 13 mission did not achieve its goal of landing on the moon, but it moved the space program forward in important ways. It built confidence within NASA that emergencies could be handled during a mission. It also led to improvements in spacecraft design and safety procedures. The people involved in the Apollo 13 mission were able to overcome the challenges they faced through a mix of training, creativity, teamwork, and bravery. These qualities are still considered essential for all NASA missions today.

GO ON →

11 **Part A**

With which statement about the Apollo 13 mission would the author **most likely** agree?

(A) It was an ideal opportunity to develop creative solutions.

(B) It failed because of a lack of adequate planning.

(C) It created a completely unnecessary risk.

(D) It was not a total failure.

Part B

Which sentence from the article **best** supports the answer to Part A?

(A) "The three men were two days into their mission and around 200,000 miles from Earth when an oxygen tank exploded on their service module." (paragraph 1)

(B) "Unfortunately, even the most careful planning had not prepared the crew for a long flight back to Earth in the lunar lander." (paragraph 3)

(C) "It was their term for a device made out of spare parts: an empty box, a breathing tube from a space suit, and even duct tape!" (paragraph 5)

(D) "The Apollo 13 mission did not achieve its goal of landing on the moon, but it moved the space program forward in important ways." (paragraph 6)

GO ON →

12 Why does the author say that "[t]he people involved in the Apollo 13 mission were able to overcome the challenges they faced through a mix of training, creativity, teamwork, and bravery"? Use specific examples from the article to support your answer.

_____

_____

_____

_____

_____

_____

Read the story "The Detour." Then answer questions 13 and 14.

The Detour

1 "Just look at that sunset straight ahead. It's like we're marching into a gigantic, crimson spaceship . . ."

2 Famished and hungry, Stuart was only half-listening to Dan, the scoutmaster. Truthfully, Stuart had never been the most accomplished scout. He didn't earn the most patches or awards, and his tent sagged like a hammock instead of forming a smartly peaked triangle like the others. But what really caused him trouble was his curiosity—he asked a lot of questions, and he was easily distracted.

3 Stuart wondered, for example, if different kinds of toasting sticks could alter a hot dog's flavor. Could it pick up the taste from whatever kind of stick was chosen? And if a stick could transfer taste, wasn't it possible for certain kinds of wood to transfer poison to a hot dog? Stuart thought perhaps he should volunteer to be the group's "Official Food Taster," where he could ensure that each stick was safe by eating one or two of the first hot dogs toasted on it. The thought made his mouth water.

4 Stuart's daydreaming continued while he followed the stretched-out line of scouts. Suddenly, Stuart's attention was caught by a rustling on the ground near the trail. Stopping, he examined the bushes. There it was again, a swirl of crackling leaves and a tiny peep. He crept closer to the sound, and a little bird flopped from one clump of bushes to another. Stuart followed the bird farther off the trail to the next bush, and then to another, but each time he drew near, the bird dragged itself farther away, as if its wing was broken. It made a distressed noise as it fluttered awkwardly from bush to bush. Then, abruptly, the bird sailed off far into the forest, and Stuart realized it had been feigning injury to lead him away from its nest. The ploy worked: Stuart was nowhere near the nest, or the trail. Even more alarming, Dan and the other scouts were gone.

GO ON →

5   Stuart inhaled deeply. The sun was sinking, and he thought how frigid the night would be if he had to sleep outside. Focusing all his senses, he heard the faint sound of running water down the hill to his right. To his left, the terrain climbed steeply up a mountain. The hike had been long, but level; they hadn't crossed any rivers or climbed a mountain on their way out, so they shouldn't need to on their way back. Then he recalled Dan's comment: "Just look at that sunset straight ahead." Stuart started walking decisively toward the setting sun.

6   About 20 minutes later, when Stuart popped like a magician into the clearing at the center of camp, Dan exclaimed with relief, "Stuart! We were really worried. We were just organizing a search party to come and find you. How did you get back to camp?"

7   Stuart explained how he used his senses and logic to figure it out. "Down to the river and up the mountain were definitely wrong, so I headed straight for the giant, red spaceship," he said.

GO ON →

13 **Part A**

What does the word **feigning** mean as it is used in paragraph 4?

(A) hiding

(B) faking

(C) causing

(D) suffering

Part B

What detail from paragraph 4 **best** helps the reader understand what **feigning** means?

(A) The bird finally flies off into the forest.

(B) The bird peeps and makes an alarmed noise.

(C) The bird leads Stuart away from the other scouts.

(D) The bird is injured and moves in an uncoordinated way.

GO ON →

14 **Part A**

Which statement **best** summarizes a central message of the story?

(A) Stress destroys good sense and logic.

(B) One's curiosity can lead to trouble.

(C) Staying organized leads to success.

(D) Animals cannot be trusted.

Part B

Which sentence from the story **best** supports the answer to Part A?

(A) "Famished and hungry, Stuart was only half-listening to Dan, the scoutmaster." (paragraph 2)

(B) "He didn't earn the most patches or awards, and his tent sagged like a hammock instead of forming a smartly peaked triangle like the others." (paragraph 2)

(C) "Suddenly, Stuart's attention was caught by a rustling on the ground near the trail." (paragraph 4)

(D) "The sun was sinking, and he thought how frigid the night would be if he had to sleep outside with no shelter or campfire." (paragraph 5)

GO ON →

Name: _____ Date: _____

Refer to the article "Apollo 13: A Galactic Challenge" and the story "The Detour"
Then answer question 15.

15 Describe the differences in the problems faced by the astronauts in
"Apollo 13: A Galactic Challenge" and Stuart in "The Detour" and how
they are resolved. Use details from the article and the story to support
your answer.

_____

_____

_____

_____

_____

_____

_____

_____

_____

_____

_____

_____

GO ON →

The following passage needs revision. Read the passage. Then answer questions 16 through 25.

Toward the end of July, Sabrina started thinking about field hockey. She would be going to the middle school in the fall, and __(1)__ goal was to make the field hockey team. To do that, she would have to start exercising.

Sabrina liked to run by __(2)__ sometimes, especially early in the morning. But if she was really going to get into shape, she needed a partner, another girl __(3)__ goal was to make the team. __(4)__ would be Abby. Sabrina and Abby had been friends since first grade. __(5)__ lived close to each other and often walked to school together.

Abby was excited about the idea when Sabrina called her, so they met at the field on Monday morning and started __(6)__ workouts. By ten o'clock, __(7)__ were exhausted. But they felt good, too. They knew that if they worked hard enough, __(8)__ be ready for the tryouts.

After two weeks, Sabrina and Abby were running four miles every day. They practiced their sprints and backward running and field hockey skills.

On the first day of school, the girls walked together. Sabrina said, "Abby, thanks for working out with me this summer. __(9)__ in the best shape ever, and I can hardly wait for tryouts. Success will be __(10)__ !"

GO ON →

16 Which answer should go in blank (1)?

(A) her

(B) hers

(C) your

17 Which answer should go in blank (2)?

(A) herself

(B) itself

(C) themselves

18 Which answer should go in blank (3)?

(A) which

(B) who

(C) whose

19 Which answer should go in blank (4)?

(A) It

(B) Her

(C) That

20 Which answer should go in blank (5)?

(A) Them

(B) They

(C) We

GO ON →

21 Which answer should go in blank (6)?

(A) they're

(B) there

(C) their

22 Which answer should go in blank (7)?

(A) both

(B) each

(C) them

23 Which answer should go in blank (8)?

(A) they'd

(B) they've

(C) they're

24 Which answer should go in blank (9)?

(A) We's

(B) We're

(C) We'are

25 Which answer should go in blank (10)?

(A) us

(B) ours

(C) our

Narrative Writing Task

Today you will read "Starship Graduate," a science fiction story. As you read and answer the questions, pay close attention to the setting and characters to help prepare you to write a narrative story.

Read the story "Starship Graduate." Then answer questions 1 through 6.

Starship Graduate

1 Gaia North listened as President Bindu Chandra addressed the graduates. Finally, she and the other fourteen-year-olds would choose more focused, high-level studies and participate as voting members of society.

2 "More than two hundred years ago," the President continued, "the starship *Jefferson* left Earth carrying thousands whose descendants would become the first humans to settle the planet Gamma X5. Now, as we enter the journey's final phase, your generation will finally realize our ancestors' dream: a truly equal, democratic society established on a new, promising world. During the next few decades, you will prepare to found a new civilization . . ."

3 After the speech, Gaia joined her friends as they crowded around tables of refreshments. Heading for a table of fruit, Gaia noticed a wall panel seemed out of alignment. Slowing to get a closer look, she realized it was a door. Curious, Gaia slipped through the opening to find herself in a storage room, and she wasn't alone.

4 A thin girl in strange clothes was hefting huge bags of flour off a pushcart. Hearing Gaia enter, she whirled, clutching her shirtfront and gasping in fear.

5 "I'm so sorry," cried the girl, "I'm not supposed to be seen, but I didn't know anyone could get in here—"

6 "You didn't do anything wrong. . . ." Gaia started to explain about the open panel, but the look of the girl stole her words. About Gaia's age, she was dressed in tattered, plain clothes. The starship travelers wore bright silks and other lush fabrics—but this girl's trousers and button-down shirt were colorless and threadbare. Most disturbing was how thin she appeared. Dark hollows sunk beneath her pale cheeks, and her wrist bones bulged under her skin.

7 "Are you ill?" Gaia asked. "Or . . . lost, or . . . My name's Gaia."

8 "I'm Tess—and I should go."

GO ON →

9 "Wait," said Gaia, grabbing the girl's arm. Tess flinched back, her eyes widening in fear.

10 "I won't hurt you—I just want to ask . . . well, I've never met anyone like you before."

11 "You're not supposed to—we usually stay out of sight."

12 "We?"

13 "Lows—jobbers like me, who live Below."

14 "Wait," said Gaia. "There's nothing below this level but storage and supplies."

15 Tess scoffed. "Who do you think does all the miserable jobs—the messy chores, the heavy lugging?" With a grunt, she heaved another sack off the cart. "Who slops the pigs and grinds the flour and picks the crops?"

16 "But that's impossible—ours is an equal society. If people knew about this—"

17 "Oh, people know," said Tess bitterly. "Your elders, those in important positions . . ."

18 "You could vote for change," said Gaia, "nominate a candidate for the next elections."

19 Tess let out an angry laugh. "You're assuming that Lows have the rights of citizens, that we can vote." Pushing her cart onto a large floor tile, she pressed her foot in the corner and the panel lowered into the Below, taking the cart, and Tessa, with it.

20 Gaia leaned against a low counter, her brain churning about what to do with this stunning revelation. She was only a recent graduate—but hadn't the President just named her class the future founders of a new civilization? She couldn't simply do nothing. Gaia took a deep breath. If she were to tell others about this, she needed more information.

21 Eyes on the floor, she walked across the tiles until she found the right one. Her heart racing, Gaia pressed the corner with her foot and descended into the Below.

GO ON →

1 **Part A**

How does the encounter with Tess affect Gaia?

(A) It makes Gaia lose confidence in the starship's mission.

(B) It decreases tension between Gaia and the President.

(C) It creates conflict over Gaia's belief in her society.

(D) It increases Gaia's desire to land on Gamma X5.

Part B

Which **two** sentences from the story, when taken together, **best** support the answer to Part A?

(A) "Gaia North listened as President Bindu Chandra addressed the graduates." (paragraph 1)

(B) "'More than two hundred years ago,' the President continued, 'the starship *Jefferson* left Earth carrying thousands whose descendants would become the first humans to settle the planet Gamma X5.'" (paragraph 2)

(C) "'Now, as we enter the journey's final phase, your generation will finally realize our ancestors' dream: a truly equal, democratic society established on a new, promising world.'" (paragraph 2)

(D) "With a grunt, she heaved another sack off the cart." (paragraph 15)

(E) "'But that's impossible—ours is an equal society.'" (paragraph 16)

(F) "Eyes on the floor, she walked across the tiles until she found the right one." (paragraph 21)

GO ON →

2 **Part A**

Which option **best** describes how the author sets the scene in the story?

(A) by providing a speech about the starship's mission

(B) by showing Gaia discovering a hidden storage room

(C) by describing the clothing worn by starship travelers

(D) by introducing a character from a secret, unequal class

Part B

Which detail from the story **best** supports the answer to Part A?

(A) "Finally, she and the other fourteen-year-olds would choose more focused, high-level studies and participate as voting members of society." (paragraph 1)

(B) "'During the next few decades, you will prepare to found a new civilization . . .'" (paragraph 2)

(C) "Gaia started to explain about the open panel, but the look of the girl stole her words." (paragraph 6)

(D) "The starship travelers wore bright silks and other lush fabrics—but this girl's trousers and button-down shirt were colorless and threadbare." (paragraph 6)

GO ON →

3 **Part A**

How does paragraph 20 contribute to the development of the story?

(A) It represents the climax.

(B) It further establishes the setting.

(C) It shows the lesson Gaia learns.

(D) It presents the resolution.

Part B

Which phrase from paragraph 20 **best** supports the answer to Part A?

(A) "... leaned against a low counter ..."

(B) "... stunning revelation."

(C) "... only a recent graduate ..."

(D) "... future founders of a new civilization ..."

GO ON →

4 **Part A**

Which **best** states a central idea in the story?

(A) Education, not hard work, is the key to success.

(B) Deeds, not words, show a leader's true beliefs.

(C) It is impossible to wipe out poverty completely.

(D) Those who seek power are often corrupt.

Part B

Which **two** details from the story, when taken together, **best** convey the central idea in Part A?

(A) "'. . . our ancestors' dream: a truly equal, democratic society . . .'" (paragraph 2)

(B) "'. . . hollows sunk beneath her pale cheeks. . .'" (paragraph 6)

(C) "'Lows—jobbers like me, who live Below.'" (paragraph 13)

(D) "'Oh, people know . . . Your elders, those in important positions . . .'" (paragraph 17)

(E) "'You could vote for change . . .'" (paragraph 18)

(F) ". . . only a recent graduate . . ." (paragraph 20)

GO ON →

5 How does Gaia's attitude change during the story? Select **three** statements from the list, and write them in the chart.

Beginning	
Middle	
End	

She is confused about how to best help Tess.

She is determined to discover more about the Lows.

She is nervous about choosing high-level studies.

She is impatient with the graduation ceremony.

She is proud to be part of the starship's mission.

She is shocked to discover things are not as they seem.

GO ON →

6   In the story "Starship Graduate," the author develops a unique setting and two very different characters. Think about the details the author uses to establish the setting and create the characters.

Write an original story about what happens when Gaia descends into the Below. In your story, be sure to use what you have learned about the setting and characters as you tell what happens next.

Write your story on a separate sheet of paper.

STOP

Answer Key

Name: _____

Question	Correct Answer	Content Focus	CCSS	Complexity
1	see below	Homophones	RL.6.1, RL.6.4, L.6.4a	DOK 1
2A	A	Idioms	RL.6.1, RL.6.4, L.6.5a	DOK 2
2B	B	Idioms	RL.6.1, RL.6.4, L.6.5a	DOK 2
3A	D	Theme	RL.6.1, RL.6.2	DOK 3
3B	C	Theme	RL.6.1, RL.6.2	DOK 2
4	D, F	Theme	RL.6.1, RL.6.2	DOK 3
5	see below	Point of View	RL.6.1, RL.6.6	DOK 3
6A	A	Context Clues: Paragraph Clues	RI.6.1, RI.6.4, L.6.4a	DOK 2
6B	C, E, F	Context Clues: Paragraph Clues	RI.6.1, RI.6.4, L.6.4a	DOK 2
7A	D	Homographs	RI.6.1, RI.6.4, L.6.4a	DOK 1
7B	B	Homographs	RI.6.1, RI.6.4, L.6.4a	DOK 1
8A	C	Author's Point of View	RI.6.1, RI.6.6	DOK 3
8B	D	Author's Point of View	RI.6.1, RI.6.6	DOK 2
9	see below	Author's Point of View	RI.6.1, RI.6.6	DOK 3
10A	C	Author's Point of View	RI.6.1, RI.6.6	DOK 3
10B	D	Author's Point of View	RI.6.1, RI.6.6	DOK 2
11A	D	Author's Point of View	RI.6.1, RI.6.6	DOK 3
11B	D	Author's Point of View	RI.6.1, RI.6.6	DOK 2
12	see below	Author's Point of View	RL.6.1, RI.6.6	DOK 3
13A	B	Context Clues: Paragraph Clues	RL.6.1, RL.6.4, L.6.4a	DOK 2
13B	A	Context Clues: Paragraph Clues	RL.6.1, RL.6.4, L.6.4a	DOK 2
14A	B	Theme	RL.6.1, RL.6.2	DOK 3
14B	C	Theme	RL.6.1, RL.6.2	DOK 2
15	see below	Compare Across Texts	W.6.9	DOK 4
16	A	Possessive Pronouns	L.6.1a	DOK 1

Question	Correct Answer	Content Focus	CCSS	Complexity
17	A	Kinds of Pronouns	L.6.1b	DOK 1
18	C	More Pronouns	L.6.1d	DOK 1
19	C	More Pronouns	L.6.1d	DOK 1
20	B	Pronouns and Antecedents	L.6.1c	DOK 1
21	C	Possessive Pronouns	L.6.1a	DOK 1
22	A	More Pronouns	L.6.1c	DOK 1
23	A	Pronoun-Verb Agreement	L.6.1c	DOK 1
24	B	Pronoun-Verb Agreement	L.6.1c	DOK 1
25	B	Possessive Pronouns	L.6.1d	DOK 1

Comprehension: Selected Response 3A, 3B, 4, 5, 8A, 8B, 9, 10A, 10B, 11A, 11B, 12, 14A, 14B,	/16	%
Comprehension: Constructed Response 12, 15	/6	%
Vocabulary 1, 2A, 2B, 6A, 6B, 7A, 7B, 13A, 13B	/10	%
English Language Conventions 16–25	/10	%
Total Unit Assessment Score	/42	%

1 Students should circle *bare* and *bear*.

5 Students should mark "something they can play with" and "a piece of artwork that reminds them of their childhood."

9 Students should underline the following sentences:
- She has been working all night.
- The air appears to be warm and humid, but she seems not to care.

12 **2-point response:** The people who worked on the Apollo 13 mission had to use their training when they moved from the service module to the lunar lander. They had actually planned for this, even though no one thought it would happen. Creativity and teamwork were needed to solve the problem of the high level of carbon dioxide. The engineers back on Earth made a "mailbox" out of extra parts to remove the carbon dioxide. The three astronauts displayed bravery after the explosion when they kept working to solve all the problems.

15 **4-point response:** In "Apollo 13: A Galactic Challenge" and "The Detour" both the astronauts and Stuart have to overcome a challenge and find their way back home. But there are a lot of differences between the two passages in how they accomplish this. "The Detour" is really just about Stuart. He gets himself into trouble by following a bird into the forest, and he has to find his own way back to camp. The other scouts aren't able to help him because they don't know he's missing. Stuart uses logic and survival skills to solve his own problem.

In contrast, in "Apollo 13: A Galactic Challenge," the astronauts did not cause the problem they faced; the explosion on the spaceship was an accident. Communication and teamwork were important because many people, on the spaceship and on Earth, had to work together to figure out how to save power, stay warm, remove carbon dioxide from the air, and get the astronauts back home. Another difference between the passages is that, unlike Stuart, the astronauts were not lost. Everyone knew where they were and what problems they were having. Like Stuart, they needed skill and training to solve their problems. But the astronauts on Apollo 13 also had to be very creative. They were facing problems that no one had ever faced before.

Name: _____

Unit 4 Assessment: Narrative Writing Task

Question	Answer	CCSS	Complexity
1A	C	RL.6.1, RL.6.3	DOK 2
1B	C, E		DOK 2
2A	A	RL.6.1, RL.6.5	DOK 2
2B	B		DOK 2
3A	A	RL.6.1, RL.6.3	DOK 2
3B	B		DOK 2
4A	B	RL.6.1, RL.6.2	DOK 3
4B	A, D		DOK 2
5	see below	RL.6.1, RL.6.3	DOK 2
6	see below	W.6.3–W.6.10 L.6.1, L.6.2, L.6.3, L.6.6	DOK 4

Comprehension 1A, 1B, 2A, 2B, 3A, 3B, 4A, 4B, 5	/10		%
Prose Constructed Response 6	/12 [WE] /3 [LC]		%
Total Narrative Writing Score	/25		%

5 Students should write the following statements in the chart:
- Beginning: She is proud to be part of the starship's mission.
- Middle: She is shocked to discover things are not as they seem.
- End: She is determined to discover more about the Lows.

6 15-point anchor paper:

The tile hummed as it slowly lowered Gaia into the unknown. Gaia clenched her muscles, bending her knees slightly and squeezing her hands into fists. She had to be ready for anything. The light dimmed as she descended, but she could still make out her surroundings. Gaia was surprised. She'd expected the underbelly of the starship to be cavernous, but it was only the size of a large room.

The tile came to a stop and Gaia stepped off as it rose back up. She seemed to be standing on a small landing platform. It must be a connection point, then, a place from which the Lows could access the rest of the ship.

The Lows. The rest of the ship. Every time it hit her—that people on the starship were living a lie—she couldn't quite believe it.

Looking for an exit, Gaia spotted a door. She found a button on the wall, and hoping it didn't require a code, gave it a push. It opened with a whoosh, and Gaia flattened herself against the wall. Slowly, she peeked around the corner.

The door had opened onto a long, grimy hallway. The paint was a greenish gray, and many of the ceiling lights were broken. Gaia stepped out and turned to the left. She walked past a number of doors, some with signs marked, "Produce Sorting Station," "Broom Closet," and "Washroom." One door, painted freshly in red, was labeled "Monitor." It was the only one with a window. Gaia peeked in, surprised to find an office decorated much like the ones on the upper levels.

Suddenly, she heard approaching footsteps. Freezing for a second, she continued walking down the hallway, trying to look like she had every business being there. Then a man and a woman came around the corner, chatting as they pushed a cart. They saw Gaia and their eyes widened in fear. They stopped, as if to let her pass.

"Hello, Monitor," said the woman, ducking her head. The man said nothing. He just stood next to the woman and looked at the floor.

So, people down here were used to visits from the upper levels—Monitors who monitored . . . what, exactly? The two workers were dressed plainly, just like Tess. Gaia noticed that their cart held cleaning supplies.

"Is there something wrong, Monitor?" the woman asked, not raising her eyes.

"Actually," said Gaia, "I do need some assistance. I'm new to the job, and I'm wondering if you could show me around a bit, maybe answer a few questions."

They both looked up for a moment, horrified. "Us?" said the man. "I'm sure that's a manager's job. We wouldn't dare—"

"Yes, I know," said Gaia, thinking on her feet, "but I only have a minute. Please?"

The fear she inspired in these people made Gaia extremely uncomfortable. But right now, it was working to her advantage. They agreed to escort her to some of the Below areas—but only those with open access. Leaving their cart by the wall, the two workers led Gaia into an elevator and down two more levels. The doors opened onto a huge public area the size of the one where Gaia had just celebrated her graduation. But size was the only similarity. Crowds of plainly clothed Lows hurried back and forth on wobbly walkways, or sat on splintery benches, resting or eating. Stairs zigzagged up the towering walls, leading to tiny apartments crammed together in the hundreds.

Gaia walked slowly through the area, mesmerized by the people and their living conditions. Did they know how everyone on the upper levels lived? Did they realize that most people up there had no idea the Below even existed? Well, that's why Gaia was here. And she wasn't going to miss a thing.

Read the story "In the Deep End." Then answer questions 1 through 5.

In the Deep End

1   "How about Thailand?" Anna asked me, spinning the globe on her desk and putting her finger down on the Southeast Asian country.

2   "I don't think anyone speaks English there," I said. "This is our first big trip abroad, so shouldn't we go somewhere a little more . . . familiar?"

3   "No way!" laughed Anna. "Where's your sense of fun, Paul? I'm sure we can get by wherever we go. We'll figure it out. And besides, people probably speak English there. Either way, this is going to be a blast. The worst thing that can happen is we'll have a little adventure, and that wouldn't be so bad, would it?" Anna gave me a smile, and I knew we were going to Thailand.

4   Anna and I had lived next door to one another since we were little. Our families were good friends, and every year we took a trip together for a few weeks during summer break. This year, our parents surprised us and said that, because we were a little older, we could try to come up with a good vacation spot for everyone. I was really excited. This was a huge treat, as well as a huge responsibility. Last year, we went to Florida and swam in the hotel pool every single day. This year I wanted to go somewhere similar, but Anna insisted we try something a bit more exotic. While I helped select a few activities, Anna planned the majority of the trip, and we soon found ourselves traveling across the globe to Bangkok, Thailand.

5   Flying always drains me, so when we first arrived in Bangkok after a grueling 17-hour flight, I was looking forward to a hamburger and a long nap, but Anna had other ideas. The first activity on the jam-packed schedule involved being immediately picked up from our hotel and driven 65 miles into the countryside to visit a Thai floating market. Anna had intentionally hidden this part of the plan from me because she knew I wasn't a fan of trying new foods, and the only water I liked was in a pool, sparkling and heated to a comfortable 86 degrees. On top of all this, I was nervous that we wouldn't be able to communicate due to the language differences.

6   The floating market made me uneasy at first. It was very crowded, and our small vessel bobbed and swayed as we made our way through the maze of boats filled with vegetables, sweets, and meats. Anna and our parents were eagerly sampling this and tasting that. They seemed to really be having a good time, but I refused to eat anything because I was determined to stay in a bad mood.

GO ON →

7 Just as my stomach began to rumble with complaint, a small boat glided up next to ours. Aboard, there was a Thai boy who appeared to be about my age. He smiled at me, holding out a giant, wild-looking fruit that was green and covered with spikes going every which way. I was about to shake my head to say no, when Anna started laughing and declared, "He won't eat it. He doesn't like adventures!"

8 I was tired of being hungry, tired of being cranky, and very tired of Anna thinking she was tougher than I am, so I reached out and took half of the spiky fruit ball. Just as I was about to bite into the strange-looking fruit, I realized it had a very strong, repulsive smell. I must have made a face because Anna let out a little giggle.

9 "Try it!" the boy said. "You'll like it."

10 I was shocked. "You speak English?" I asked the boy.

11 "Of course!" he replied. "You should give the fruit a chance. It's called a durian. It's delicious. They say only the smartest and boldest traveler will try it."

12 I could feel Anna watching me, so I quickly took a big bite of the fruit. To my surprise, I actually liked it. The flavor was unlike any I had experienced before. As the boy's boat started to drift ahead, he gave me a thumbs up.

13 Later that night back at our hotel, Anna asked, "So, was it *that* bad?"

14 "What do you mean?" I responded.

15 "The boat ride, the food, the whole day. Are you happy we came to Thailand?"

16 I could tell she was curious to hear my thoughts on our unique day. I think she was impressed that I was really diving into our trip, rather than wading in the shallow end.

17 "Me? Oh, yeah. I think this is going to be our best summer trip yet," I answered a bit timidly.

18 "Good," Anna smiled. "That makes me feel better. After all, you've always been the brave one."

GO ON →

Name: _____ Date: _____

1 **Part A**

What is the meaning of the word **repulsive** as it is used in paragraph 8?

(A) disgusting

(B) unique

(C) weird

(D) sweet

Part B

Which detail from paragraph 8 **best** helps the reader understand the meaning of **repulsive**?

(A) "... the strange-looking fruit ..."

(B) "... realized it had a very strong ..."

(C) "... must have made a face ..."

(D) "... let out a little giggle."

2 Read the sentence from paragraph 16.

| I could tell she was curious to hear my thoughts on our unique day. |

Circle a denotation and a connotation for the word **unique** as it is used in the sentence.

Denotation	Connotation
one-of-a-kind	unpleasant
commonplace	remarkable
run-of-the-mill	customary
widespread	exhausting

GO ON →

3 **Part A**

Which statement **best** describes the relationship between Anna and Paul?

(A) Anna and Paul work as a team to make most decisions.

(B) Paul does not allow Anna to control their relationship.

(C) Anna and Paul challenge each other to learn new things.

(D) Anna's influence over situations sometimes annoys Paul.

Part B

Which detail from the story **best** supports the answer to Part A?

(A) "'I don't think anyone speaks English there,' I said. 'This is our first big trip abroad, so shouldn't we go somewhere a little more . . . familiar?'" (paragraph 2)

(B) "Our families were good friends, and every year we took a trip together for a few weeks during summer break." (paragraph 4)

(C) "I was about to shake my head to say no, when Anna started laughing and declared, 'He won't eat it. He doesn't like adventures!'" (paragraph 7)

(D) "I was tired of being hungry, tired of being cranky, and very tired of Anna thinking she was tougher than I am, so I reached out and took half of the spiky fruit ball." (paragraph 8)

GO ON →

4 **Part A**

Which statement **best** describes the main conflict in the story?

(A) Paul can never get enough sleep.

(B) Paul does not like to try new food.

(C) Paul tries to resist new experiences.

(D) Paul is constantly getting teased by Anna.

Part B

Which detail from the story **best** supports the answer to Part A?

(A) ". . . we could try to come up with a good vacation spot for everyone." (paragraph 4)

(B) "This was a huge treat, as well as a huge responsibility." (paragraph 4)

(C) ". . . after a grueling 17-hour flight, I was looking forward to a hamburger and a long nap . . ." (paragraph 5)

(D) ". . . I refused to eat anything because I was determined to stay in a bad mood." (paragraph 6)

5 Which **two** effects does the character of the boy at the market have on the plot?

(A) He teaches Paul to be stubborn.

(B) He proves that Paul has no sense of adventure.

(C) He convinces Paul to return to his hotel.

(D) He helps Paul learn to relax and enjoy his vacation.

(E) He shows that Paul is bold enough to respond to a challenge.

(F) He explains to Paul how people travel in foreign countries.

GO ON →

Read the article "A Brief History of Football." Then answer questions 6 through 10.

A Brief History of Football

1 One day in 1892, William "Pudge" Hefelfinger recovered a fumble and ran for a touchdown to win a football game against the Pittsburgh Athletic Club. That effort earned "Pudge" a $500 bonus (plus $25 for travel expenses), and he became the first paid professional football player in America. But how did football begin, and how did it eventually become a professional sport?

The Beginning of the "American" Game

2 College teams had been playing football for at least 23 years before Pudge's professional debut. On November 6, 1869, two college teams clashed in New Jersey for the first time in history. Rutgers University beat the team from what is now known as Princeton University on their home field with a score of 6 to 4.

3 After this game, other colleges in the eastern United States started to play football. In the 1880s, Walter Camp, the football coach of Yale University, developed the football field that is used today. He drew up the measurements and the markings. He also set down the rules for the game.

4 Probably the most important rule involved how the players moved the ball down the field. Camp's idea used several tries, called "downs," for each team to move the ball a certain number of yards toward the goal. Today's football is played using this rule of "downs."

Where It All Began

5 Football has roots as far back as 206 B.C.E., during the Han Dynasty of China. The emperor's birthday was celebrated with an ancient ball game called Tsu Chu.

6 Later, in the 1200s, men from rival villages in England played a similar game. They would try to hold onto an inflated cow bladder and run it into the center of the opposing village. To stop the advance, violent tackles took place between teams. Players would constantly get injured, and some even died. The game was so violent that the king outlawed the sport in the city of London. But Rome wasn't built in a day—football remained popular throughout the country. People outside of London continued to play, and the sport continued to develop.

7 The game became more popular in 1623. By that time, the game involved players running back and forth on a field rather than to and from their villages. They touched the ball only with their feet.

GO ON →

8 At Rugby College in England, the game changed once again. In 1823, a Rugby College player named William Ellis surprised everyone during a game. Instead of kicking the ball, he picked it up and raced across the goal line. The crowd loved this bold move, and it started the game that we now know as rugby. The American game of football eventually developed from rugby.

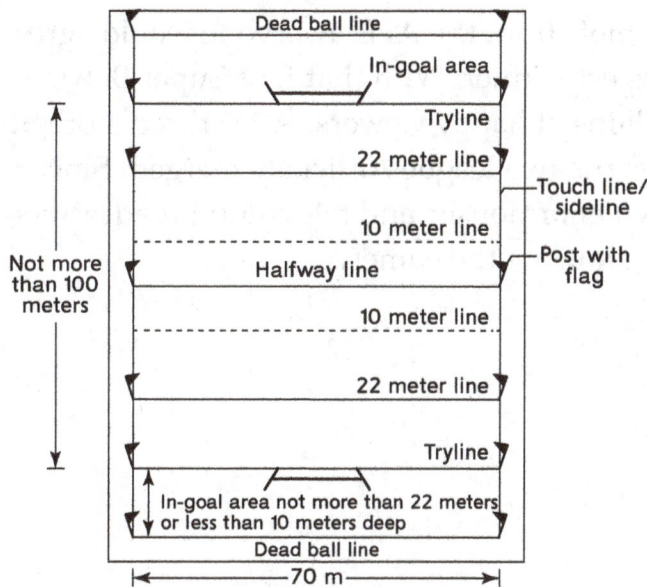

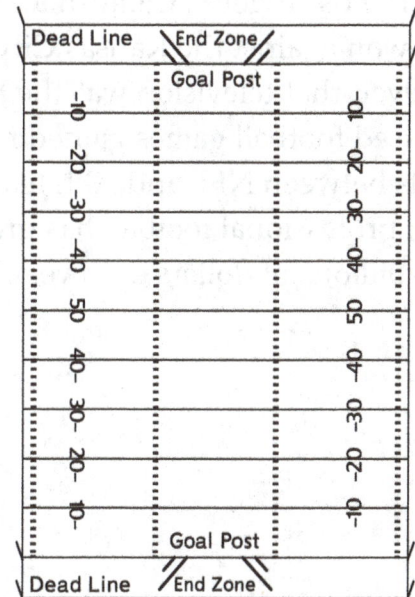

A Rugby Field   **A Football Field**

Football Across America

9 The American colonists from England created their own football-like games, but today's form of football did not catch on across the rest of the nation until that first organized college game between Rutgers and Princeton. After that, colleges and athletic associations across the East and Midwest took up the sport. Over the next 20 years, the game spread from the east coast of the United States to the west. Excitement about the sport grew, and so did the number of fans.

10 The first college championship game was played in the Rose Bowl in California in 1902. But by 1905, football had become a dangerous sport, and too many players were getting injured. To protect the health of the players, President Theodore Roosevelt considered banning football. No one wanted that, so the rules of the game changed yet again, with most of the changes related to the line of scrimmage. The line of scrimmage is an invisible line across the field that marks where the last play ended and where the next play begins. It was the place where opposing players collided and most injuries occurred.

GO ON →

11 By 1920, the American Professional Football Association was born. Two years later, it became the National Football League, now known as the NFL. In 1960, another league, called the American Football League (AFL), formed. With two powerful leagues, no one really knew whose teams were the best, so in 1967 the Super Bowl was created to answer that question. The first Super Bowl game was held in Los Angeles, California, where Wisconsin's Green Bay Packers from the NFL won against the Kansas City Chiefs from the AFL. Everyone would agree, however, that television was the biggest winner. With that first Super Bowl, televised football games gained millions of happy viewers. After three more Super Bowls between NFL and AFL teams, the two leagues officially merged. Since that time, professional football has grown enormously, and television broadcasters earn billions of dollars each year by showing the games.

GO ON →

6 **Part A**

What does the word **rival** mean as it is used in paragraph 6?

(A) ancient

(B) competing

(C) trendy

(D) welcoming

Part B

Which word from paragraph 6 **best** supports the answer to Part A?

(A) villages

(B) similar

(C) inflated

(D) opposing

7 Read the sentence from paragraph 6.

> But Rome wasn't built in a day—football remained popular throughout the country.

What does the phrase **Rome wasn't built in a day** mean as it is used in the sentence?

(A) Football is a popular sport played every day in Rome.

(B) The modern sport of football began one day in Rome.

(C) People stopped playing football in England after it was outlawed.

(D) It took a long time for football to develop into the game it is today.

GO ON →

8 **Part A**

Which statement **best** illustrates the author's attitude toward football?

(A) Football is popular, but it is a very risky sport.

(B) Without football, television networks would fail.

(C) Football has been ruined by high salaries and huge television profits.

(D) Colleges and universities kept football alive when no one wanted to watch it.

Part B

Which sentence from the article **best** supports the answer to Part A?

(A) "That effort earned 'Pudge' a $500 bonus (plus $25 for travel expenses), and he became the first paid professional football player in America." (paragraph 1)

(B) "After that, colleges and athletic associations across the East and Midwest took up the sport." (paragraph 9)

(C) "But by 1905, football had become a dangerous sport, and too many players were getting injured." (paragraph 10)

(D) "Everyone would agree, however, that television was the biggest winner." (paragraph 11)

9 Using the diagrams of the rugby field and the football field, mark **one** box that is true for **each** statement.

	Rugby	Football	Both
A flag marks the midway line.	☐	☐	☐
Numbers count down from the middle of the field.	☐	☐	☐
The field is longer than it is wide.	☐	☐	☐
The field is divided into equal 10-yard lengths.	☐	☐	☐

GO ON →

10 **Part A**

What does the author suggest was the effect of having two separate football leagues, the NFL and the AFL?

(A) The two leagues became competitive.

(B) Television broadcasters became rich.

(C) American football adopted formal rules.

(D) Football players became professional athletes.

Part B

Which sentence from the article **best** supports the answer to Part A?

(A) "No one wanted that, so the rules of the game changed yet again, with most of the changes related to the line of scrimmage." (paragraph 10)

(B) "Two years later, it became the National Football League, now known as the NFL." (paragraph 11)

(C) "With two powerful leagues, no one really knew whose teams were the best, so in 1967 the Super Bowl was created to answer that question." (paragraph 11)

(D) "Since that time, professional football has grown enormously, and television broadcasters earn billions of dollars each year by showing the games." (paragraph 11)

GO ON →

Today you will read an article and a story about scientific discovery.

Read the article "Credit When Due." Then answer questions 11 and 12.

Credit When Due

1 Alfred Wegener was a German scientist known during his lifetime for studying the weather and exploring the polar ice caps. His four trips to Greenland were so difficult that many considered him more of an adventurer than a scientist. The days on the polar ice were long and dark. Wegener was collecting data and reading research reports from a wide variety of scientific fields. His interests ranged from rocks and fossils to tornadoes and meteorites.

2 In 1915, at the age of 35, Wegener published "The Origin of Continents and Oceans." In this book, he noted that the North and South American land masses seemed to fit together with the European and African continents. He argued that the continents used to be connected, but they had drifted away from each other over millions of years. He could not explain how or why, but he proposed that it might be due to the force of Earth's rotation. In another paper, he reasoned that ocean rifts were pushing the continents apart. Wegener called his idea the theory of "continental drift."

3 However, the idea was quickly rejected by other scientists. They said that Wegener did not consider things like erosion or fully explain how continents could move. Most thought that the similar outline of the continents was just a coincidence. They said land masses could move up or down due to volcanic activity, but they could not drift around the planet's surface.

4 Some have argued that Wegener's theories were victims of timing and bias. His book was first published in Germany during World War I, so it received little attention. Also, his research was supported by the German government, which was blamed for the war. Others point out that the tone of Wegener's papers was too rigid and assertive. Wegener's poor command of English did not allow him to defend his theories against criticism by British and American scientists. In all likelihood, his peers would not have accepted his theories without data from technologies that were decades away from being developed.

5 While he gathered more data and sought wider acceptance for his theories, Wegener taught at the University of Hamburg and organized research trips to Greenland. In 1930, he led his fourth expedition there. His team of 14 scientists wanted to gather information on Arctic weather and the thickness of the ice

GO ON →

sheet. However, severe weather caused Wegener to make a risky supply run. He died at the age of 50 from overexertion and extreme cold.

6 After Wegener's death, scientists continued to gather data on geology and global weather patterns. New tools such as computers, sonar, radar, and satellites allowed for more precise measurements of surface movements and volcanic vents on the ocean floor. Emerging fields like paleomagnetism provided strong support for the theory of continental drift. Then, in 1953, geologists found rock samples in India that clearly matched samples from continents in the southern hemisphere. These discoveries and many others confirmed Wegener's earlier ideas. His theory of continental drift led to the modern, widely accepted theory of plate tectonics.

7 Today, Wegener is considered the father of an entire field of geophysics. Although his discoveries were not accepted during his lifetime, modern scientists give him credit for many important ideas. He conceived of complex movements of Earth's continents and weather systems, often from very limited data. Alfred Wegener was a great thinker whose discoveries have stood the test of time.

GO ON →

11 Write the number 1, 2, 3, or 4 on the lines below to put the details from the article in sequential order.

_____ Wegener argued that the continents were once connected but had drifted apart.

_____ Wegener's research was supported by the field of study called paleomagnetism.

_____ Wegener's theory of the continents being connected was proven to be true.

_____ Wegener wanted to study the ice sheets in the Arctic.

12 Why was Alfred Wegener's theory of continental drift initially rejected and eventually accepted by the scientific community? Use details from the article to support your answer.

_____

_____

_____

_____

_____

_____

_____

GO ON →

Read the story "The Age of Discovery." Then answer questions 13 and 14.

The Age of Discovery

1 Claire was ambivalent about visiting her Grandma Bonnie—she was excited to see her, but it would be the first time she had visited her grandmother since she had moved into the retirement home. Claire couldn't visualize her vivacious grandma in a facility like that. She pictured a gloomy interior with tiny windows, ugly carpeting, and battleship-gray paint.

2 Claire had magical memories of her grandmother. She wasn't the type of person who showered Claire with gifts and cookies, but she could tell a whopper of a story. How many grandmothers could say they had worked as a spy, a firefighter, a chef, and a hot-air balloon pilot? Grandma Bonnie could go on for hours about close calls behind enemy lines, or catering for royalty, or near-fatal disasters at 5,000 feet. How could she be content in a retirement home, such a quiet, ordinary, slow-paced place?

3 Arriving at the Sunnyside Senior Living Center, Claire was surprised to find it handsomely landscaped, with vividly colored flowers and an expansive, park-like front lawn. Several residents were outside reading or golfing on a perfectly manicured putting green. Inside, the place was bright and airy, with lots of activity. Instead of grim TV rooms full of people sitting quietly in front of game shows or talk shows, there was cheery laughter while knitting, painting, and even dancing.

4 She found her grandmother in a comfy, sunlit corner, tapping intently on a laptop.

5 "Hello, my dear!" Grandma Bonnie chirped. "I'll be right with you—just have to finish this thought."

6 "Take your time." Noticing a stack of papers, Claire asked, "Is this your current project?"

7 "Yes, but it needs a lot of help—you can be my editor!"

8 Claire expected to read a story about Grandma Bonnie the spy, young and fluent in French. Instead, she found a fairy story about tiny, childlike creatures with unbreakable shells or glow-in-the-dark wings, struggling to save their corner of the forest from imminent destruction.

9 Grandma Bonnie finished typing with a triumphant flourish and turned to Claire. "It's like science fiction for children," she explained. Then, tapping a thick stack of science and nature magazines, she added, "I draw inspiration from these.

GO ON →

When I discover something remarkable about a squid, or an insect, or a hummingbird, I imagine what would happen if people had that characteristic, and then I put them into challenging situations and see what happens."

10 "This is incredible," Claire murmured, engrossed in the story.

11 "It's a hoot," said Grandma Bonnie. "The publisher says the first book is selling like wildfire, and she's pestering me for another one."

12 Claire was bewildered.

13 "It's been a while, dear. I wrote the first book last autumn, and I guess it's proven popular with parents who want to teach their kids about science, while stoking their imagination simultaneously."

14 "You published a book since I last saw you?" Claire whispered in disbelief.

15 Grandma Bonnie nodded with a humble smile and offered, "It's all about discovery. Discovery leads to more discoveries, which leads to the joy of even more discovery. That's the path I followed my entire life, so I guess it's working for others, too."

16 Overflowing with awe and pride, Claire decided then and there that she would be spending a lot more time at the Sunnyside Senior Living Center. Though being an editor wasn't as glamorous as being a spy or a balloon pilot, Grandma Bonnie would make it a grand adventure.

GO ON →

13 **Part A**

Read the sentence from paragraph 1.

> Claire couldn't visualize her vivacious grandma in a facility like that.

The word **vivacious** comes from the Latin root *vivax*, which means "long-lived or high-spirited." What does **vivacious** mean?

(A) athletic

(B) friendly

(C) energetic

(D) elderly

Part B

Which **two** details from the story **best** support the answer to Part A?

(A) "... wasn't the type of person who showered Claire with gifts and cookies ..." (paragraph 2)

(B) "... could go on for hours about close calls behind enemy lines, or catering for royalty ..." (paragraph 2)

(C) "She found her grandmother in a comfy, sunlit corner, tapping intently on a laptop." (paragraph 4)

(D) "... finished typing with a triumphant flourish and turned to Claire." (paragraph 9)

(E) "'The publisher says the first book is selling like wildfire ...'" (paragraph 11)

(F) "... nodded with a humble smile and offered ..." (paragraph 15)

GO ON →

14 **Part A**

What is Claire's initial reason for wanting to avoid going to the retirement home?

(A) She thinks it will be a gloomy place.

(B) She is afraid to see Grandma Bonnie.

(C) She is sad to see her grandmother getting older.

(D) She is upset that there are so few interesting activities.

Part B

Which sentence from the story **best** shows how Claire's problem is resolved?

(A) "How many grandmothers could say they had worked as a spy, a firefighter, a chef, and a hot-air balloon pilot?" (paragraph 2)

(B) "How could she be content in a retirement home, such a quiet, ordinary, slow-paced place?" (paragraph 2)

(C) "Arriving at the Sunnyside Senior Living Center, Claire was surprised to find it handsomely landscaped, with vividly colored flowers and an expansive, park-like front lawn." (paragraph 3)

(D) "She found her grandmother in a comfy, sunlit corner, tapping intently on a laptop." (paragraph 4)

GO ON →

Name: _____ Date: _____

Refer to the article "Credit When Due" and the story "The Age of Discovery." Then answer question 15.

15 Science plays an important role in both "Credit When Due" and "The Age of Discovery." Explain how scientific discovery opened new possibilities for Alfred Wegener and Grandma Bonnie. Use details from both texts to support your answer.

_____

_____

_____

_____

_____

_____

_____

_____

_____

_____

_____

_____

_____

GO ON →

The following passage needs revision. Read the passage. Then answer questions 16 through 25.

(1) The Hubble telescope has changed our understanding of space. (2) It is an telescope that orbits Earth. (3) It is outside Earth's atmosphere. (4) For this reason, it takes most clear pictures than other telescopes. (5) Around 1600, Italian scientist Galileo used a telescope. (6) Even the earliest astronomers wanted to see deep into space. (7) Early telescopes were worser than telescopes of today. (8) With Hubble, astronomers can see farer into space than ever before.

(9) The National Aeronautics and Space Administration (NASA) launched the Hubble Space Telescope in 1990. (10) Pictures from this telescope have helped astronomers learn the age of the universe. (11) These is an important advance for astronomy. (12) Today, the bestest calculations place the age of the universe at 13 to 14 billion years old.

(13) The Hubble telescope is one of NASA's most importantest tools. (14) It has been repaired in space a couple of times. (15) The more recent service was done in 2009. (16) For now, this telescope is wonderful. (17) But someday the Hubble will stop working, and it will not be repaired again.

GO ON →

16 How can sentence 2 **best** be written?

(A) It is a telescope that orbits Earth.

(B) It is this telescope that orbits Earth.

(C) It is any telescope that orbits Earth.

(D) It is some telescope that orbits Earth.

17 How can sentence 4 **best** be written?

(A) For this reason, it takes more clearer pictures than other telescopes.

(B) For this reason, it takes clearer pictures than other telescopes.

(C) For this reason, it takes most clear pictures than other telescopes.

(D) For this reason, it takes clearly pictures than other telescopes.

18 Which sentence uses a proper adjective?

(A) Sentence 2

(B) Sentence 3

(C) Sentence 4

(D) Sentence 5

19 How can sentence 7 be written correctly?

(A) Early telescopes were worse than telescopes of today.

(B) Early telescopes were badder than telescopes of today.

(C) Early telescopes were baddest than telescopes of today.

(D) Early telescopes were more worse than telescopes of today.

GO ON →

20 What is the correct way to write sentence 8?

Ⓐ With Hubble, astronomers can see more far into space than before.

Ⓑ With Hubble, astronomers can see farther into space than before.

Ⓒ With Hubble, astronomers can see fartherer into space than before.

Ⓓ With Hubble, astronomers can see more farther into space than before.

21 How can sentence 11 **best** be written?

Ⓐ This is a important advance for astronomy.

Ⓑ This is an important advance for astronomy.

Ⓒ Those is an important advance for astronomy.

Ⓓ Those is a important advance for astronomy.

22 What is the correct way to write sentence 12?

Ⓐ Today, the best calculations place the age of the universe at 13 to 14 billion years old.

Ⓑ Today, the bester calculations place the age of the universe at 13 to 14 billion years old.

Ⓒ Today, the most best calculations place the age of the universe at 13 to 14 billion years old.

Ⓓ Today, the more better calculations place the age of the universe at 13 to 14 billion years old.

23 How can sentence 13 be written correctly?

Ⓐ The Hubble telescope is one of NASA's importanter tools.

Ⓑ The Hubble telescope is one of NASA's most important tools.

Ⓒ The Hubble telescope is one of NASA's more importanter tools.

Ⓓ The Hubble telescope is one of NASA's importantest tools.

GO ON →

24 What is the correct way to write sentence 15?

(A) The recenter service was done in 2009.

(B) The recentest service was done in 2009.

(C) The most recent service was done in 2009.

(D) The most recentest service was done in 2009.

25 Which sentence contains a predicate adjective?

(A) Sentence 14

(B) Sentence 15

(C) Sentence 16

(D) Sentence 17

STOP

Research Simulation Task

Today you will research inventions, inventors, and the creative process. You will read an article titled "Imagination Expo." Then you will read an article titled "Useless Inventions" and text from a presentation titled "Accidental Inventions." As you review these sources, you will gather information and answer questions about inventions so you can write an essay.

Read the article titled "Imagination Expo." Then answer questions 1 through 3.

Imagination Expo

1   Where can you go to meet hundreds of inventors from all over the world and see a thousand wonderful, weird, or wacky inventions? You can find it all at the International Exhibition of Inventors. Held for five days each April in Geneva, Switzerland, it is the biggest exhibition of its kind in the world.

2   For more than 40 years, inventors have traveled to this event to show off their unique creations. Some come for social reasons, eager to network with other inventors like themselves. Some come to find people who might be willing to invest money in their products. Others come looking for partners to help them with manufacturing their products or marketing them to the public. Besides individual inventors, small companies, research institutes, and universities also attend.

3   Strolling through the event is fascinating. One display might have an incredibly useful invention designed to make life easier. Exhibited next to it might be an invention created merely to make life more fun.

4   Only those inventions that have been patented are allowed to enter. Getting a patent is no guarantee an invention will be popular. It does, however, mean that the inventor has been granted property rights by the government. For a specified period of time, the inventor has the sole right to make, use, or sell their invention. The inventor also has the right to sue anyone who tries to "infringe upon," or copy, their property. Whether any of the products on display at the exhibition will eventually turn a profit is anyone's guess.

GO ON →

5 **The Amazing and Amusing**

Many of the inventions found at this exhibition are intended to make life better, safer, or more convenient. In the past, these have included lamps that can create their own power. The exhibition hall has seen a wind generator that needs only the slightest breeze to produce power. One display featured a protective suit for people working in toxic or hazardous environments.

6 One young inventor from China has designed a set of special see-through parachutes for assisting airplanes in emergency landings. A couple from Spain shows off bags made out of tissue for placing over fruit and vegetables during unexpectedly cold or bad weather.

7 A German company has created a bicycle-like vehicle equipped with large, colorful rubber balls instead of wheels. The inventors dreamed it up as a fun way to exercise. A woman from South Korea offers a device for people who have trouble tying their shoelaces. This device attaches to the shoelaces and ties them with a single touch. A man from Iran displays his "super smart boots." These collect information on everything from air temperature and humidity to the wearer's blood pressure. A French company is busy marketing battery-powered roller skates that attach to the soles of people's shoes. Put on a pair and you can move as fast as nine miles per hour.

8 Other inventions are less practical, but more fun. One example is a portable backrest. This item is designed for the weary—lean back on it and you can rest without sitting down. The idea for the device came from studying how kangaroos use their tails.

9 What else is on display? What *isn't*? There are mouthwash-dispensing toothbrushes. There's a hands-free umbrella that doubles as a pair of suspenders. Other inventors are showing off super-fast sock driers or one-handed bottle openers. There's even a device that makes changing sheets faster by flipping over and revolving the entire bed.

GO ON →

10 **The Winners**

Although many of the inventions are fun and entertaining, the serious ones usually take home the top prizes. For example, the 2009 winner is from Romania. This inventor created a mobile truck scanner that allows border guards and custom checkers to scan the interior of trucks much more quickly and thoroughly. In 2012, a Hong Kong company won the gold medal for creating a robotic glove designed to give stroke victims the ability to use their hands again. The 2014 exhibition winners took away two gold medals—one for a new diabetes testing system and one for a new way for healthcare workers to measure bacteria on skin and ensure their hands are germ free.

11 So, what do all these inventors have in common? According to one participant, inventors are dreamers who also know how to follow through on their ideas and turn them into something tangible. And if you visit the annual International Exhibition of Inventors, you'll see the results of this particular combination of skills: dreams made real.

GO ON →

1 **Part A**

What is the meaning of the word **tangible** as it is used in paragraph 11 of "Imagination Expo"?

(A) easy

(B) actual

(C) useful

(D) tireless

Part B

Which detail from paragraph 11 **best** supports the answer to Part A?

(A) ". . . in common?"

(B) ". . . know how to follow through . . ."

(C) ". . . particular combination of skills . . ."

(D) ". . . dreams made real."

GO ON →

2 **Part A**

Which **best** describes the overall structure of "Imagination Expo"?

(A) The text groups inventions into categories according to general purpose.

(B) The text contrasts entertaining inventions with prize-winning inventions.

(C) The text presents information about the exhibition in order of importance.

(D) The text provides step-by-step instructions for how to enter the exhibition.

Part B

Which **two** sentences from the article **best** support the answer to Part A?

(A) "For more than 40 years, inventors have traveled to this event to show off their unique creations." (paragraph 2)

(B) "For a specified period of time, the inventor has the sole right to make, use, or sell their invention." (paragraph 4)

(C) "Many of the inventions found at this exhibition are intended to make life better, safer, or more convenient." (paragraph 5)

(D) "A German company has created a bicycle-like vehicle equipped with large, colorful rubber balls instead of wheels." (paragraph 7)

(E) "Other inventions are less practical, but more fun." (paragraph 8)

(F) "The idea for the device came from studying how kangaroos use their tails." (paragraph 8)

GO ON →

3 Look at the list of inventions described in "Imagination Expo" and decide whether they are **Practical, Mostly for Fun,** or **Prize-Winning**. Write **each** invention in the appropriate location in the chart.

Practical	Mostly for Fun	Prize-Winning

Inventions

Mobile truck scanner	Robotic glove for stroke victims
Mouthwash-dispensing toothbrush	Portable backrest
Smart boots that collect information	Device that measures skin bacteria
Lamp that creates its own power	Wind generator powered by a breeze
One-handed bottle opener	

GO ON →

Read the article "Useless Inventions." Then answer questions 4 through 6.

Useless Inventions

1 From Bell's telephone to Babbage's computer, Edison's light bulb to Farnsworth's television, these inventions ended up making lives better, easier, safer, and more convenient. Sometimes, however, an invention is fun but totally useless. There's a name for that: *chindogu*, which is Japanese for "strange tools."

2 A chindogu must conform to certain rules. It cannot be useful, or sold to the public. It must be made from simple tools and cannot be patented. No fancy computer parts are allowed. In fact, true chindogu are simply observed and admired. Anything that ends up being useful or handy is disqualified.

3 **The Original Inventor**
The person behind chindogu is a Japanese man named Kenji Kawakami. He was a magazine editor when, about 25 years ago, he designed something for pure entertainment: a pair of glasses that funneled eye drops directly into the eyes. Readers absolutely loved it. In the decades since then, Kawakami has invented more than 700 odd creations that he explains in several books. His playful inventions have been featured in everything from magazine articles to museum displays.

4 With thousands of fans worldwide, Kawakami has inspired others to start building and designing. Learning from his offbeat creations, inventors ages 10 to 70 have produced their own weird, whimsical items.

5 **Chindogu Examples**
A peek at some of Kawakami's inventions shows just how unhelpful a chindogu can be. For example, his electric rotating spaghetti fork winds up the noodles—which would be great, except for one thing: it flings spaghetti sauce everywhere. Then there's the hat made for taking 360-degree photographs. Made out of eight disposable cameras, it allows you to snap photos while you—the hat-wearer—spin around. Again, nice, if moving didn't blur the pictures. Or you might try using Kawakami's solar-powered flashlight, but wait—if there's enough light to power the solar cells, why do you need a flashlight?

GO ON →

6   Kawakami has also created wearable inventions that you might not want to wear. He designed a pair of shoes and socks with built in mops for cleaning the floor as you move (with special models for cats, dogs, and babies). He also invented a two-way shoe that faces both directions so you can slide it on no matter which way you go. He even made a tie that doubles as an umbrella.

7   Kawakami's silly ideas also include a set of glasses with built-in fans for cutting onions without tears. He created a double-headed toothbrush for brushing the top and bottom teeth at the same time, and alarm-clock headphones that wake you up without bothering anyone else. His trickiest invention to date is probably his security padlock. This item has 20 numbered dials that would take 3.2 trillion years to figure out and open.

8   Although a chindogu product may not be useful, the process of creating it may be. In fact, school and universities throughout the world now teach students about chindogu as a way to encourage creativity and new thinking patterns. This is certainly true for Kawakami, who makes no money from his inventions. He just enjoys experimenting, and creating unique things. And owning the official title "world's first *chindogist*" isn't bad either.

GO ON →

4 **Part A**

Read the sentence from paragraph 4 of "Useless Inventions."

> Learning from his offbeat creations, inventors ages 10 to 70 have produced their own weird, whimsical items.

What does the word **whimsical** mean as it is used in the sentence?

- (A) tricky
- (B) amusing
- (C) confusing
- (D) thoughtful

Part B

Which detail from the article **best** supports the answer to Part A?

- (A) "... better, easier, safer ..." (paragraph 1)
- (B) "... must conform to certain rules." (paragraph 2)
- (C) "... useful or handy ..." (paragraph 2)
- (D) "... playful inventions ..." (paragraph 3)

GO ON →

5 **Part A**

How does paragraph 3 contribute to the development of ideas in "Useless Inventions"?

(A) It shows that the idea for chindogu is fairly recent.

(B) It notes that the concept of chindogu comes from Japan.

(C) It illustrates how popular useless inventions can be.

(D) It provides background information on Kenji Kawakami's early life.

Part B

Which paragraph from the article **best** supports the answer to Part A?

(A) paragraph 2

(B) paragraph 4

(C) paragraph 5

(D) paragraph 7

GO ON →

6 **Part A**

How does the author of "Useless Inventions" support the idea that making chindogu can be useful?

(A) by describing the skills involved in developing chindogu

(B) by describing the rules to which all chindogu must conform

(C) by describing some of Kawakami's most famous chindogu

(D) by contrasting chindogu with more helpful inventions

Part B

Which sentence from the article **best** supports the answer to Part A?

(A) "From Bell's telephone to Babbage's computer, Edison's light bulb to Farnsworth's television, these inventions ended up making lives better, easier, safer, and more convenient." (paragraph 1)

(B) "It must be made from simple tools and cannot be patented." (paragraph 2)

(C) "He also invented a two-way shoe that faces both directions so you can slide it on no matter which way you go." (paragraph 6)

(D) "In fact, school and universities throughout the world now teach students about chindogu as a way to encourage creativity and new thinking patterns." (paragraph 8)

GO ON →

Read the text from the presentation "Accidental Inventions." Then answer questions 7 and 8.

The following information is part of a presentation on how lucky mistakes resulted in some very important inventions.

[slide 1]

Accidental Inventions
Discovering Something Without Intending To

[slide 2]

Stumbling Upon Something New

Inventors typically spend years studying, researching, and experimenting to create something new and unique. Now and then, however, inventions don't go quite as planned. Sometimes, inventors make an unexpected and exciting discovery that takes their research in a different direction. Other times, inventors experience some fortunate event in their everyday lives that triggers a brilliant idea.

The following food additive, fastener, and medical device were discovered by accident.

GO ON →

[slide 3]

#1: A Sweet Surprise

- **Inventors:** The Johns Hopkins University researchers Constantin Fahlberg and Ira Remsen

- **When it happened:** 1879

- **What they were trying to make:** a new use for coal tar

- **What happened:** After a frustrating day in the lab, Fahlberg came home and had dinner with his family. He immediately noticed that his wife's biscuits tasted much sweeter than usual. His wife had used the same recipe she always did, so what caused the distinctive flavor? It turned out to be the chemical on his hands. Fahlberg named the substance *saccharin* after the word *saccharine* ("sugary") and was soon mass producing his artificial sweetener. Saccharin tasted similar to sugar, but it was cheaper, easier to produce, and calorie-free.

- **What they ended up inventing:** saccharin

[slide 4]

#2: Burrs, Dogs, and Socks

- **Inventor:** Swiss electrical engineer George de Mestral

- **When it happened:** 1955

- **What he was trying to do:** take his dog for a walk

- **What happened:** After taking his dog for a walk outside, de Mestral examined the burrs (prickly seeds) clinging to his socks and pants, as well as to his dog's fur. How exactly did the burrs stick to cotton or hair? Could he make a new type of fastener that imitated the burrs? After some trial and error, de Mestral ended up using two strips—one with tiny hooks and one with fuzzy loops. Few paid much attention to the strange-looking invention until the 1960s when NASA began using the material in their flight suits. Soon enough, everyone from skiers to scuba divers saw the advantage of de Mestral's invention.

- **What he ended up inventing:** hook-and-loop fastener

GO ON →

[slide 5]

#3: The Beat Goes On

- **Inventors:** Canadian electrical engineer John Hopps
- **When it happened:** 1951
- **What he was trying to make:** a device for restoring body temperature
- **What happened:** Hopps knew that people who got too cold suffered from a condition called hypothermia. If body temperature was not restored in time, the heart could stop. As Hopps tried to use radio frequencies to increase body temperature, he accidentally discovered that a stopped heart could be restarted with an electrical pulse. He used this knowledge to develop the world's first external pacemaker. Although Hopps's invention was big and uncomfortable for patients to use, it led to the smaller, internal pacemakers that many people rely on today.
- **What he ended up inventing:** external pacemaker

GO ON →

7 **Part A**

Read the sentence from slide 3 of "Accidental Inventions."

> His wife had used the same recipe she always did, so what caused the distinctive flavor?

What is the meaning of the word **distinctive** as it is used in the sentence?

Ⓐ having a confusing quality

Ⓑ having a distasteful quality

Ⓒ having a suspicious quality

Ⓓ having a different quality

Part B

Which detail from slide 3 is a clue to the meaning of **distinctive** in Part A?

Ⓐ "... a frustrating day in the lab ..."

Ⓑ "... much sweeter than usual."

Ⓒ "... had used the same recipe ..."

Ⓓ "... the chemical on his hands."

GO ON →

8 Part A

Which option **best** states the author's purpose in "Accidental Inventions"?

(A) to interest the reader in learning more about inventions

(B) to inform the reader about inventions that developed by accident

(C) to entertain the reader with funny stories about unexpected inventions

(D) to show the reader that most accidental inventions are developed by scientists

Part B

Which sentence from the presentation **best** supports the answer to Part A?

(A) "Inventors typically spend years studying, researching, and experimenting to create something new and unique." (slide 2)

(B) "Sometimes, inventors make an unexpected and exciting discovery that takes their research in a different direction." (slide 2)

(C) "Soon enough, everyone from skiers to scuba divers saw the advantage of de Mestral's invention." (slide 4)

(D) "Hopps knew that people who got too cold suffered from a condition called hypothermia." (slide 5)

GO ON →

Name: _____ Date: _____

Refer to the articles "Imagination Expo" and "Useless Inventions," and the text from the presentation "Accidental Inventions." Then answer questions 9 and 10.

9 Mark **one** idea that is introduced in all three texts. Then circle **one** sentence from **each** text that supports this idea.

Idea	
_____	Inventing something useful requires skill in science, engineering, technology, or medicine.
_____	Creating a chindogu can accidentally lead to inventing something useful.
_____	The most important quality needed to develop an invention is creativity.
_____	Invention is a creative process that involves skill, imagination, persistence, and execution.

"Imagination Expo"	"Useless Inventions"	"Accidental Inventions"
"Others come looking for partners to help them with manufacturing their products or marketing them to the public."	"Sometimes, however, an invention is fun but totally useless."	"Inventors typically spend years studying, researching, and experimenting to create something new and unique."
"A French company is busy marketing battery-powered roller skates that attach to the soles of people's shoes."	"A peek at some of Kawakami's inventions shows just how unhelpful a chindogu can be."	"After some trial and error, de Mestral ended up using two strips—one with tiny hooks and one with fuzzy loops."
"Although many of the inventions are fun and entertaining, the serious ones usually take home the top prizes.	"Kawakami has also created wearable inventions that you might not want to wear."	"Soon enough, everyone from skiers to scuba divers saw the advantage of de Mestral's invention."
"According to one participant, inventors are dreamers who also know how to follow through on their ideas and turn them into something tangible."	"In fact, school and universities throughout the world now teach students about chindogu as a way to encourage creativity and new thinking patterns."	"As Hopps tried to use radio frequencies to increase body temperature, he accidentally discovered that a stopped heart could be restarted with an electrical pulse."

GO ON →

Grade 6 • Unit Assessment • Unit 5

10 You have read about inventions by reading two articles, "Imagination Expo" and "Useless Inventions," and text from a presentation titled "Accidental Inventions." Write an essay that compares the main purposes of the three sources and discusses the methods each author uses to accomplish this purpose. Be sure to use evidence from all three sources to support your response.

Write your essay on a separate sheet of paper.

Name: _____

Question	Correct Answer	Content Focus	CCSS	Complexity
1A	A	Context Clues: Cause and Effect	RL.6.1, RL.6.4, L.6.4a	DOK 2
1B	C	Context Clues: Cause and Effect	RL.6.1, RL.6.4, L.6.4a	DOK 2
2	see below	Connotation and Denotation	RL.6.1, RL.6.4, L.6.5c	DOK 2
3A	D	Character, Setting, Plot: Problem and Solution	RL.6.1, RL.6.3	DOK 3
3B	D	Character, Setting, Plot: Problem and Solution	RL.6.1, RL.6.3	DOK 2
4A	C	Character, Setting, Plot: Problem and Solution	RL.6.1, RL.6.3	DOK 3
4B	D	Character, Setting, Plot: Problem and Solution	RL.6.1, RL.6.3	DOK 2
5	D, E	Character, Setting, Plot: Cause and Effect	RL.6.1, RL.6.5	DOK 2
6A	B	Context Clues: Definitions and Restatements	RI.6.1, RI.6.4, L.6.4a	DOK 2
6B	D	Context Clues: Definitions and Restatements	RI.6.1, RI.6.4, L.6.4a	DOK 2
7	D	Adages and Proverbs	RI.6.1, RI.6.4, L.6.5a	DOK 2
8A	A	Author's Point of View	RI.6.1, RI.6.6	DOK 2
8B	C	Author's Point of View	RI.6.1, RI.6.6	DOK 2
9	see below	Text Feature: Diagrams	RI.6.1, RI.6.7	DOK 1
10A	A	Text Structure: Cause and Effect	RI.6.1, RI.6.5	DOK 2
10B	C	Text Structure: Cause and Effect	RI.6.1, RI.6.5	DOK 2
11	see below	Text Structure: Sequence	RI.6.1, RI.6.5	DOK 2
12	see below	Text Structure: Cause and Effect	RI.6.1, RI.6.5	DOK 2
13A	C	Word Origins	RL.6.1, RL.6.4, L.6.4b	DOK 1
13B	B, D	Word Origins	RL.6.1, RL.6.4, L.6.4b	DOK 1
14A	A	Character, Setting, Plot: Problem and Solution	RL.6.1, RL.6.3	DOK 2
14B	C	Character, Setting, Plot: Problem and Solution	RL.6.1, RL.6.3	DOK 2
15	see below	Compare Across Texts	W.6.9	DOK 4
16	A	Articles and Demonstrative Adjectives	L.6.1	DOK 1

Answer Key

Name: _____

Question	Correct Answer	Content Focus	CCSS	Complexity
17	B	Adjectives That Compare	L.6.1	DOK 1
18	D	Adjectives	L.6.1	DOK 1
19	A	Comparing with *Good* and *Bad*	L.6.1	DOK 1
20	B	Adjectives That Compare	L.6.1	DOK 1
21	B	Articles and Demonstrative Adjectives	L.6.1	DOK 1
22	A	Comparing with *Good* and *Bad*	L.6.1	DOK 1
23	B	Comparing with *More* and *Most*	L.6.1	DOK 1
24	C	Comparing with *More* and *Most*	L.6.1	DOK 1
25	C	Adjectives	L.6.1	DOK 1

Comprehension: Selected Response 3A, 3B, 4A, 4B, 5, 8A, 8B, 9, 10A, 10B, 11, 12, 14A, 14B	/16	%
Comprehension: Constructed Response 12, 15	/6	%
Vocabulary 1A, 1B, 2, 6A, 6B, 7, 13A, 13B	/10	%
Grammar, Mechanics, Usage 16–25	/10	%
Total Unit Assessment Score	/42	%

2 Students should circle the following:
- **Denotation:** one-of-a-kind
- **Connotation:** remarkable

9 Students should mark the boxes as follows:
- Rugby: A flag marks the midway line.
- Football: Numbers count down from the middle of the field. The field is divided into equal 10-yard lengths.
- Both: The field is longer than it is wide.

11 Students should write the following numbers: 1, 3, 4, 2.

12 **2-point response:** Alfred Wegener's theory was not accepted during his lifetime mainly because he couldn't explain how the continents could move. He was also a victim of bad timing. After he died, people invented many technologies like radar, sonar, satellites and computers could be used to measure the movement of the continents. Also, scientists started doing experiments in geology and paleomagnetism. For example, geologists found rocks in India that were the same as rocks from continents in the southern hemisphere. These experiments supported Wegener's theory.

15 **4-point response:** Scientific discovery is an important theme in both texts. In "Credit When Due," Alfred Wegener was a German scientist who made an important discovery. By looking at a map, he realized that the continents used to fit together but had drifted apart over millions of years. Wegener spent his time "collecting data and reading research reports from a wide variety of scientific fields."

In "The Age of Discovery," Grandma Bonnie uses science and nature magazine articles as the basis for her children's stories. Grandma Bonnie's interest in science opens up the possibility of doing another job, after a lifetime of other interesting jobs. In this case, it's helping her to become a successful author. It also gives children the chance to learn about nature and science in a fun and creative way.

Both Alfred Wegener and Grandma Bonnie loved to learn and to explain the world through observation. Grandma Bonnie just liked to discover and learn for the joy of it. This is why she did so many different and interesting jobs. Wegener went to Greenland to study the weather and the ice, even though it was a very dangerous place. He could have just stayed in Germany to teach in the University, but he kept going to Greenland to learn more and get information that would support his theory.

Answer Key

Question	Answer	CCSS	Complexity
1A	B	RI.6.1, RI.6.4, L.6.4a	DOK 2
1B	D		DOK 2
2A	A	RI.6.1, RI.6.5	DOK 2
2B	C, E		DOK 2
3	see below	RI.6.1, RI.6.2, RI.6.5	DOK 1
4A	B	RI.6.1, RI.6.4, L.6.4a	DOK 2
4B	D		DOK 2
5A	C	RI.6.1, RI.6.5	DOK 2
5B	B		DOK 2
6A	A	RI.6.1, RI.6.2	DOK 2
6B	D		DOK 2
7A	D	RI.6.1, RI.6.4, L.6.4a	DOK 2
7B	B		DOK 2
8A	B	RI.6.1, RI.6.6	DOK 2
8B	B		DOK 2
9	see below	RI.6.1, RI.6.3	DOK 3
10	see below	RI.6.1, RI.6.6, RI.6.9 W.6.2, W.6.4–W.6.10 L.6.1, L.6.2, L.6.3, L.6.6	DOK 4

Unit 5 Assessment: Research Simulation Task

Comprehension 2A, 2B, 3, 5A, 5B, 6A, 6B, 8A, 8B, 9	/12	%
Vocabulary 1A, 1B, 4A, 4B, 7A, 7B	/6	%
Prose Constructed Response 10	/4 [RC] /12 [WE] /3 [LC]	%
Total Research Simulation Score	/37	%

3 Students should complete the chart as follows:
- Practical—Smart boots that collect information; Lamp that creates its own power; Wind generator powered by a breeze
- Mostly for Fun—Mouthwash-dispensing toothbrush; One-handed bottle opener; Portable backrest
- Prize-Winning—Mobile truck scanner; Robotic glove for stroke victims; Device that measures skin bacteria

9 Students should mark/circle the following answers in the chart:
  - Idea: Invention is a creative process that involves skill, imagination, persistence, and execution.
  - "Imagination Expo": "According to one participant, inventors are dreamers who also know how to follow through on their ideas and turn them into something tangible."
  - "Useless Inventions": "In fact, school and universities throughout the world now teach students about chindogu as a way to encourage creativity and new thinking patterns."
  - "Accidental Inventions": "Inventors typically spend years studying, researching, and experimenting to create something new and unique."

10 19-point anchor paper:

Although all three sources center on the topic of inventions, each text has a different purpose and focus. The article "Imagination Expo" describes what it's like to attend the annual International Exhibition of Inventors in Geneva, Switzerland. The author's main purpose is to highlight this exhibition and show how it brings together a wide variety of inventions. To accomplish this purpose, the author sums up the history of the exhibition and describes inventors' reasons for attending. In paragraph 2, the author mentions some of these reasons: to network with other inventors; to seek out investors; or to find manufacturing and marketing partners. The author highlights the exhibition by describing it as if the reader is actually there: "Strolling through the event is fascinating. One display might have an incredibly useful invention . . ." (paragraph 3). This "stroll" is continued throughout the article as the author describes some of the actual inventions that have been displayed in the past.

The inventions are organized by three major types. The section "The Amazing and Amusing" presents inventions that "are intended to make life better, safer, or more convenient," (paragraph 5) and those that "are less practical, but more fun" (paragraph 8). Some of the more practical inventions described here are a wind generator powered by a slight breeze and a device for people who have trouble tying their shoes. In the more fun category are examples like a portable backrest and a super-fast socks drier. In the section "The Winners," the author presents the third major type of invention, "the serious ones usually take home the top prizes" (paragraph 10). Examples in this category include a mobile truck scanner and a new diabetes testing system.

The author's purpose in "Useless Inventions" is to introduce the topic of chindogu and why it has become so popular. To accomplish this task, the author uses several methods. The article begins by noting famous, helpful inventions and contrasting these with an invention that serves no functional purpose. The author then describes the rules that every invention must meet in order to be called a chindogu: "A chindogu must conform to certain rules. It cannot be useful, or sold to the public. It must be made from simple tools, and cannot be patented" (paragraph 2). In the section "The Original Inventor," the author describes magazine editor Kenji Kawakami and how, just for fun 25 years ago, he invented a pair of eyeglasses that funneled eye drops into a person's eyes. Surprisingly, the magazine's readers loved the invention, prompting Kawakami to invent more than 700 others. He has also inspired thousands of fans to try inventing chindogu. The author helps readers understand what a truly useless invention is like by giving details. So most of the article describes actual chindogu, beginning each description with something that sounds useful—then going on to show why it's really not. For example, there's a rotating spaghetti fork that can twist up your pasta, but then flings it all over the place. In closing, the author notes that while the inventions might be useless, they inspire people to be creative and to think in new and different ways.

Answer Key

Name: _____

The main purpose of "Accidental Inventions" is to highlight some inventions that were developed by accident. The author accomplishes this by first noting that sometimes, "inventions don't go quite as planned," or other times, inventors have a random everyday experience "that triggers a brilliant idea" (slide 2). The author's method of illustrating this concept is to summarize three examples. In "A Sweet Surprise," a researcher comes home from the lab and sits down to dinner with his family. When his wife's biscuits taste unusually sweet, he realizes his hands have transferred a chemical he'd been experimenting as a substitute for coal tar. He had accidentally discovered an artificial sweetener. "Burrs, Dogs, and Socks" involves an everyday inspiration. When an engineer tries to remove burrs from his dog's fur, he starts wondering what makes them stick. This inspires him to see if he can reproduce this effect. The result is the hook-and-eye fastener. As in "A Sweet Surprise," the third example, "The Beat Goes On," presents a scientist who when trying to invent one thing, ends up inventing something different. An electrical engineer is trying to find a way to treat hypothermia by using radio frequencies to raise body temperature. He accidentally discovers that this process can restart the heart. He uses this knowledge to invent the first pacemaker.

Read the article "Bonsai: Art Through the Ages." Then answer questions 1 through 5.

Bonsai: Art Through the Ages

1   Take a visit to the garden center at the nearest home improvement store and you will likely find a display full of miniature trees in shallow, decorative pots. These are bonsai trees, and you can purchase one for a relatively low price. But understanding the true craft of *bonsai* requires more than a quick purchase at the garden center.

2   The tradition of growing bonsai trees began in China over 1,000 years ago, but it was the Japanese who made it into an art. Japanese bonsai masters have written many books about how to choose the best tree, how to care for it, and how to shape it into a visually pleasing form. If done correctly, a bonsai tree can outlive the person who originally planted it. The most famous examples are believed to be over 600 years old. This means a single bonsai tree can be carefully tended to by generations of bonsai masters.

3   But what exactly is a bonsai, and how is it different from an ordinary tree? A bonsai actually begins its life like any other tree. It is either grown from a seed or collected from the wild when it is still fairly young. But the growth of a bonsai tree is carefully controlled so that a fully mature bonsai reaches a height of less than 60 inches. Bonsai trees are kept small by restricting the roots in a shallow clay pot. Water and light are manipulated to encourage or limit the growth of leaves. The Japanese place a greater value on bonsai trees that resemble full-grown trees with thick trunks and finely shaped branches.

4   Many bonsai trees are considered living masterpieces. In Japan, some are known by name. These are as valuable as the most famous paintings or sculptures. Unlike other art forms, however, bonsai trees are prized because of the ongoing effort to keep them healthy and pleasing to the eye. Caring for them is particularly difficult as they are normally displayed outdoors and exposed to rain, heat, frost, and wind.

5   To truly appreciate the skill that goes into nurturing a bonsai tree, consider the process from start to finish. Some bonsai trees are grown from seeds, but real masters prefer to work with trees that are found in a natural setting. Rocky cliffs and sea walls are ideal because the roots are shallow and exposed, making it easier to remove the trees. Also, the steady wind from the sea often bends and weathers the trunk, giving the tree more character. Some bonsai masters reject

GO ON →

thousands of trees before choosing one to harvest. Beginners are encouraged to use commercially grown seedlings because it is hard to keep harvested trees alive. Damage to the root system and sensitivity to change can make harvested trees very fragile.

6 Once a tree is selected, it is transplanted into a low clay pot. The size, shape, and color of the pot influence the overall artistic value of the bonsai. Roots are trimmed closely to fit in the pot. The outermost roots are vital for collecting water and nutrients from the soil, so new bonsai trees often struggle to survive after they are transplanted. Once a tree is established in its new pot a few years later, it is time to begin shaping it.

7 There are many tools and techniques for shaping a bonsai tree. Some branches and leaves are trimmed. The trunk and remaining branches are wrapped with copper wire to form a variety of shapes or styles. Each of these styles is well known by students of bonsai. For example, some trees bend one way, then sweep back over the pot as if they are growing over a lake or shoreline. Others are trained to curve gracefully over the edge of the pot. This is called the "cascade," or *kengai*, style.

8 Bonsai masters have also developed many techniques to make trees appear to be old and weathered. These include *jin* and *shari*, or scarring the branches or trunk so they die and turn gray. These techniques make the tree look like it has had to struggle to survive. The result is more visually appealing and more reflective of nature.

9 Growing a bonsai tree is a long-term process that requires a mix of knowledge, practice, and patience. The entire process of growing a tree to maturity can take decades. What to do at each step along the path follows complex, ancient rules. Everything, from the choice of tree species to its final display in a garden, is governed by tradition and artistic considerations. Any false action along the way can result in aesthetic failure or the death of the tree. On the other hand, since growing a bonsai tree can take so long, people who take an active interest have plenty of time to learn the craft.

GO ON →

1 **Part A**

Read the sentences from paragraph 3.

> Bonsai trees are kept small by restricting the roots in a shallow clay pot.

The origin of the word **restricting** is the Latin root *strict,* which means "tight." What does the word **restricting** mean?

(A) limiting something

(B) eliminating something

(C) changing the size of something

(D) affecting the appearance of something

Part B

Which phrase from paragraph 3 **best** helps to explain what **restricting** means?

(A) "... carefully controlled ..."

(B) "... fully mature bonsai ..."

(C) "... resemble full-grown trees ..."

(D) "... finely shaped branches."

GO ON →

2 **Part A**

Read the sentence from paragraph 9.

> Everything, from the choice of tree species to its final display in a garden, is governed by tradition and artistic considerations.

The origin of the word *govern* is the Greek word *kybernan,* which means "to steer." What does the word **governed** mean?

(A) chosen

(B) developed

(C) controlled

(D) shown

Part B

Which word from paragraph 9 **best** supports the answer to Part A?

(A) process

(B) rules

(C) action

(D) failure

3 The author describes the steps that a bonsai master takes to raise a bonsai tree. Write a number from 1–5 next to each step to show the correct sequence.

_____ The master begins shaping the tree.

_____ The master chooses a tree to harvest.

_____ The master transplants the tree into a pot.

_____ The master lets the tree establish itself.

_____ The master trims the roots of the tree.

4 The author explains the different techniques used to raise a bonsai tree. Draw a line from each technique on the left to its effect on the right.

Technique	Effect
putting the bonsai in a shallow clay pot	makes the tree more appealing
wrapping the trunk and branches in copper wire	forms a variety of shapes and styles
scarring the branches and trunk so they die and turn gray	carries a risk that the tree will die
harvesting a bonsai from its natural setting	keeps the tree small

GO ON →

5 **Part A**

Which sentence **best** states the central idea of the article?

(A) It takes many years to grow a bonsai tree, so bonsai masters must have patience.

(B) Growing a bonsai tree is an art form that requires great effort and skill to learn properly.

(C) Bonsai masters use techniques, such as *jin* and *shari,* to make the trees appear weathered.

(D) Caring for a bonsai tree is a challenge because it is exposed to harsh weather conditions.

Part B

Which sentence from the article **best** supports the answer to Part A?

(A) "Also, the steady wind from the sea often bends and weathers the trunk, giving the tree more character." (paragraph 5)

(B) "Damage to the root system and sensitivity to change can make harvested trees very fragile." (paragraph 5)

(C) "The result is more visually appealing and more reflective of nature." (paragraph 8)

(D) "Any false action along the way can result in aesthetic failure or the death of the tree." (paragraph 9)

GO ON →

Read the article "Bapu: The Father of a Nation." Then answer questions 6 through 10.

Bapu: The Father of a Nation

1   It's difficult to picture young Mohandas Gandhi as a schoolboy in India in 1882. He was not a strong athlete, or a particularly talented student. In fact, one high school teacher reported that he was "good at English, fair in Arithmetic and weak in Geography; conduct very good, handwriting." He often read the classic Indian stories of *Shravana* and *King Harishchandra*, which stressed the importance of truth, love, and duty. At 13, as was the custom in India at the time, Mohandas was married to a 14-year-old neighbor. He was so innocent that the event seemed to him just an opportunity for "wearing new clothes, eating sweets and playing with relatives."

2   Mohandas eventually moved to London to study law. There, he joined a philosophical society that promoted the idea of universal brotherhood. Members of this group studied a number of essential Buddhist and Hindu literary works. Gandhi eventually earned a law degree and moved back to India. He was not very successful because he didn't like to argue with witnesses during a trial. By this time, he had four sons with his wife. In an effort to support his growing family, he moved to South Africa at the age of 24.

3   At that time, both India and South Africa were part of the British Empire. Britain controlled trade and collected taxes from a large number of overseas territories. If a person bought cloth, spices, tea, salt, or many other goods around 1900, they were likely produced by low-paid workers in one of Britain's many colonies.

4   In South Africa, Gandhi experienced tremendous prejudice and discrimination. Indians were treated as second-class citizens, with no voting rights and daily public humiliations. During this time, Gandhi was reading many books about human rights. One Russian writer, Leo Tolstoy, had a particularly strong influence on him. Tolstoy wrote a letter to Gandhi in 1908 saying that India could only overthrow colonial rule if they used love and passive resistance as weapons. Gradually, Gandhi began to develop his own ideas of non-violent protest. Soon he led a number of public protests over travel restrictions, voting rights, and compulsory registration—a system that allowed white South Africans to control Indian travel and trade.

GO ON →

5   In 1915, Gandhi returned to India. He was 46 years old and had gained the title *Mahatma*, or "Great Soul." He could have retired to a quiet life of minor legal work. Instead, he set to the task of separating his homeland from the largest, most powerful empire in the world. Gandhi was soon named the leader of an Indian nationalist party whose aim was complete independence from Britain. He instilled, through teaching and careful selection of party leaders, his ideas of non-violent action. By this time, he had refined the idea and given it the Sanskrit term *satyagraha*. He loosely translated this to "truth force." Gandhi believed that Indians could not defeat the British through armed conflict. Instead, peaceful resistance and civil disobedience would bring attention to the inequality and injustice in the country. Other nations would put pressure on Britain to give India independence.

6   One of the greatest applications of *satyagraha* was the "Salt March" of 1930. Gandhi led thousands of followers on a 250-mile march to a salt factory in the coastal town of Dandi. There, they made their own salt, in defiance of a British law that taxed all salt production and sale in the country. This injustice was felt deeply by all Indians, rich and poor, and motivated many to join the peaceful protest. Gandhi was thrown in prison, but the passion of the people had been ignited, and the salt march caused millions of Indians to resist other rules they considered unfair. A few weeks later, soldiers attacked hundreds of defenseless salt marchers. Many knew that the relationship between Britain and its Indian subjects would never be repaired.

7   Gandhi employed a range of tools in his various campaigns. He was imprisoned and released many times. He rejected imported British goods such as cloth, spinning his own simple clothing out of local cotton. He also fasted, denying himself food for up to three weeks. His beloved status among all Indian social and religious groups forced the authorities to accept social and political change in order to end the fast and save his life. Gandhi drifted away from formal political parties, but he continued to fight for women's rights, social equality, religious tolerance, and many other causes. India eventually gained independence from Britain in 1947.

8   During his lifetime, Gandhi said many memorable things. His words have reached such a level of admiration and repetition that many are considered universal truths. Two of his most popular proverbs are "You must be the change you wish to see in the world" and "An eye for an eye only ends up making the whole world blind." Gandhi's principle of non-violent action influenced many later civil rights leaders, including Martin Luther King Jr., and South Africa's Nelson Mandela. In India, Gandhi is referred to simply as *Bapu*, or "father."

GO ON →

6 Part A

Read the sentence from paragraph 7.

> Gandhi drifted away from formal political parties, but he continued to fight for women's rights, social equality, religious tolerance, and many other causes.

What does the word **tolerance** mean as it is used in the sentence?

(A) belief

(B) authority

(C) community

(D) acceptance

Part B

Select **two** words from the sentence that help the reader understand the meaning of **tolerance**.

(A) drifted

(B) formal

(C) political

(D) fight

(E) rights

(F) equality

7 What is the meaning of the adage "You must be the change you wish to see in the world" in paragraph 8?

(A) You have to take time to learn new skills.

(B) You should always try to experience new things.

(C) You need to act if you want to make a difference.

(D) You will be strong if you act in a peaceful manner.

GO ON →

8 Read the sentence from paragraph 3.

> At that time, both India and South Africa were part of the British Empire.

Why does the author introduce the idea that India and South Africa were colonies of Britain?

Ⓐ It explains why Gandhi fought for women's rights.

Ⓑ It explains how India was able to rid itself of foreign rulers.

Ⓒ It explains the cause of the inequalities that Indians experienced.

Ⓓ It explains the reason why Gandhi wanted to move to South Africa.

9 Part A

Which statement **best** describes an unexpected effect of British rule in India?

Ⓐ It discouraged the poor from seeking an education.

Ⓑ It created a common cause among the classes.

Ⓒ It allowed many to move to other countries.

Ⓓ It led to an increased production of salt.

Part B

Which sentence from the text **best** supports the answer to Part A?

Ⓐ "In an effort to support his growing family, he moved to South Africa at the age of 24." (paragraph 2)

Ⓑ "In South Africa, Gandhi experienced tremendous prejudice and discrimination." (paragraph 4)

Ⓒ "There, they made their own salt, in defiance of a British law that taxed all salt production and sale in the country." (paragraph 6)

Ⓓ "This injustice was felt deeply by all Indians, rich and poor, and motivated many to join the peaceful protest." (paragraph 6)

GO ON →

10 The author describes several events in Gandhi's life that led to his gaining the respect of the people in India. Put the events in the correct sequence by writing a number from 1–5 next to each event.

_____ Leads public protests in South Africa

_____ Becomes the leader of the nationalist party

_____ Reads several books about human rights

_____ Fasts and gives up all British goods

_____ Develops the idea that success will come through non-violent protest

GO ON →

Today you will read an article and a poem about living creatures' relationship with the environment.

Read the article "The Uncertain Fate of the Gateway Pacific Coal Terminal." Then answer questions 11 and 12.

The Uncertain Fate of the Gateway Pacific Coal Terminal

Background

1   As the world population increases, so does the demand for natural resources. Fortunately, new technologies and innovations have allowed companies in the United States to extract vast new coal and oil deposits in Pennsylvania, Wyoming, and North Dakota. The challenge, then, becomes transporting these deposits to refineries and to willing buyers. Although some of these resources are used in the United States, much of it is exported to Europe and Asia. This is particularly true for coal. Many of China's factories and power plants are fueled by coal.

2   Oil, gas, and coal companies are always searching for the most effective way to move their products from their source to refineries and shipping terminals. Most oil and gas used in the United States or shipped to Europe is sent to refineries in Louisiana and Texas. Coal and oil are shipped to China from ports in the northwestern states like Oregon and Washington, or from the west coast of Canada. But as coal companies began to produce more coal for China, they realized that there were not enough ports on the West Coast to ship it overseas. They began to look for other places to build ports.

Proposal

3   One location coal companies are considering is Cherry Point, near the city of Bellingham, Washington. They want to build a large shipping port at Cherry Point. They call it the Gateway Pacific terminal. If the port is built, long trains full of coal and oil would travel to Washington from Wyoming and North Dakota. At Cherry Point, the coal and oil would be loaded onto huge container ships that would then sail to China. If completed as planned, the Gateway Pacific terminal would be the largest coal exporting facility in the United States. It would ship 48 million tons of coal a year to China. Coal companies say that building and running the port would provide many jobs in Washington, at mines in the Midwest, and along the rail lines.

GO ON →

4   However, critics of the Gateway Pacific terminal have raised a number of important issues. Communities next to the railways are concerned about the number of coal trains that will pass through their communities. They fear these trains will cause a lot of noise and traffic delays. They could also block emergency vehicles. Health officials point out that coal dust from the trains can cause respiratory problems for people along the rail lines. Some people also argue that the economic benefits from the port will be minimal. They say the number of full-time jobs after the terminal is built will be fairly small. They also claim that most of the profit from exports will remain in the hands of a small number of people. In other words, Washington State would get some jobs and tax income, but most of the money would go to coal and oil companies in other states.

5   The greatest critics of the proposed Gateway Pacific terminal are environmental groups. Environmentalists argue that the mining, transport, and burning of fossil fuels like coal, oil, and gas is destroying the environment and causing climate change. They say that we should invest in renewable energies like solar, water, and wind power. One opponent of Gateway Pacific notes, "If we were shipping teddy bears to China instead of coal, most of the noise and traffic issues would probably be acceptable. But we'd be shipping coal, which directly contributes to climate change. This negatively affects everyone on the planet."

6   The fate of the Gateway Pacific terminal is uncertain. Completing the project will require the cooperation of local, state, and national governments, private companies, and the public. There are many strong arguments on both sides. The decision-making process is long and complex. Because we live in a democratic society, the course of action will not be settled until everyone has had a chance to be heard.

GO ON →

11 **Part A**

Which statement **best** expresses the main idea of the section titled "Background"?

(A) China is one of the world's largest producers of coal today.

(B) Coal companies are still considering the effect of using other ports in the United States.

(C) Using natural resources from new deposits presents the challenge of transporting it to factories.

(D) The United States would not be able to extract natural resources without the help of new technologies.

Part B

Which sentence from the "Background" section **best** supports the answer to Part A?

(A) "Fortunately, new technologies and innovations have allowed companies in the United States to extract vast new coal and oil deposits in Pennsylvania, Wyoming, and North Dakota." (paragraph 1)

(B) "Many of China's factories and power plants are fueled by coal." (paragraph 1)

(C) "Most oil and gas used in the United States or shipped to Europe is sent to refineries in Louisiana and Texas." (paragraph 2)

(D) "But as coal companies began to produce more coal for China, they realized that there were not enough ports on the West Coast to ship it overseas." (paragraph 2)

GO ON →

12 Explain how the author uses a cause-and-effect text structure in the article. Use key details from the article to support your answer.

_____

_____

_____

_____

_____

_____

_____

GO ON →

Read the poem "The Polar Bear's Home." Then answer questions 13 and 14.

The Polar Bear's Home

1   Cast your eyes far to the north,
And see a thousand suns striding forth.
In the Arctic world of never-night,
A polar bear hides white on white.
5   My mother is searching for a home,
In this icy region where we roam,
Now growing hungry and forlorn,
For me, her cub, recently born.

We needed help so long ago
10   *To keep the ice cap's glow of snow.*
But while we still have icy land,
The time to act is now at hand.

In a cold that makes you shiver,
She scoops a salmon from a river.
15   With a swipe of her giant paw,
A three-inch nail in every claw.
My father's bigger, almost a ton!
Forty miles an hour he'll run.
But mother can be very still
20   When she's waiting for a kill.
Hours on ice to get a seal,
She tries to catch our favorite meal,
But now the sun burns far too bright,
Icebergs melting out of sight.

GO ON →

25 There is no place to make our den,
     And when the winter comes—what then?
     The seals are gone, and soon the fish,
     To find some food, we only wish.
     The ice that's left is but a glint,
30 It melts away without a hint.
     And now across the Arctic dome,
     The bears like me have lost our home.

*   We needed help so long ago*
*   To keep the ice cap's glow of snow.*
35 *But while we still have icy land,*
     The time to act is now at hand.

GO ON →

13 Read lines 1–4 from the poem.

> Cast your eyes far to the north,
> And see a thousand suns striding forth.
> In the Arctic world of never-night,
> A polar bear hides white on white.

What is the effect of the hyperbole used in these lines?

(A) It compares eyes to a thousand suns.

(B) It emphasizes the strength of the sun.

(C) It exaggerates the color of a polar bear.

(D) It gives human qualities to a polar bear.

GO ON →

14 **Part A**

Which sentence **best** expresses the theme of the poem?

(A) There is hope even in dark times.

(B) Climate change is destroying nature.

(C) One creature's life touches many lives.

(D) Hunting in the wild is a great challenge.

Part B

Select **two** pairs of lines from the poem that **best** support the answer to Part A.

(A) "Now growing hungry and forlorn, / For me, her cub, recently born." (lines 7 and 8)

(B) "In a cold that makes you shiver, / She scoops a salmon from a river." (lines 13 and 14)

(C) "With a swipe of her giant paw, / A three-inch nail in every claw." (lines 15 and 16)

(D) "My father's bigger, almost a ton! / Forty miles an hour he'll run." (lines 17 and 18)

(E) "But mother can be very still / When she's waiting for a kill." (lines 19 and 20)

(F) "There is no place to make our den, / And when the winter comes— what then?" (lines 25 and 26)

GO ON →

Name: _____ Date: _____

Refer to the article "The Uncertain Fate of the Gateway Pacific Coal Terminal" and the poem "The Polar Bear's Home." Then answer question 15.

15 What central idea from "The Uncertain Fate of the Gateway Pacific Coal Terminal" is also expressed in "The Polar Bear's Home"? Use details from the texts to support your answer.

_____

_____

_____

_____

_____

_____

_____

_____

_____

_____

_____

_____

_____

_____

_____

_____

GO ON →

Grade 6 • Unit Assessment • Unit 6

The following passage needs revision. Read the passage. Then answer questions 16 through 21.

A scientific study completed ___(1)___ proves that dark chocolate is good for your heart and your overall health. That is good news for people who love chocolate. But ___(2)___ wonder where chocolate comes from? It is a fascinating story.

Chocolate is made from cocoa beans, which grow on trees. Cocoa trees grow ___(3)___ in the hottest parts of the world, which are located ___(4)___ the Equator.

The first people to harvest cocoa beans were the Aztecs in Mexico, although they used the beans for money ___(5)___ than they used them for food. Cocoa trees grew in northern parts of South America, too, and eventually spread to Brazil.

Today, cocoa beans are also grown in tropical parts of Africa, especially the Ivory Coast and Mali. You ___(6)___ find chocolate that comes from anywhere else.

GO ON →

16 Which answer should go in blank (1)?

(A) recent

(B) recenter

(C) recently

17 Which answer should go in blank (2)?

(A) don't you not

(B) don't you ever

(C) don't you never

18 Which answer should go in blank (3)?

(A) best

(B) better

(C) goodly

19 Which answer should go in blank (4)?

(A) nearer

(B) nearly

(C) near

20 Which answer should go in blank (5)?

(A) oftener

(B) more often

(C) more oftenly

21 Which answer should go in blank (6)?

(A) can hardly

(B) can't hardly

(C) can hardly not

GO ON →

The following passage needs revision. Read the passage. Then answer questions 22 through 25.

(1) Cocoa trees can reach a height of 50 feet, but they are usually pruned to about 20 feet. (2) Each cocoa tree produces thousands of blossoms and 20 to 30 fruits per year. (3) The fruits are heavy. (4) They grow next to the trunk.

(5) The fruits look like chubby cucumbers about 6 to 10 inches long. (6) The fruit's hard shell turns from green to yellow. (7) Then the shell turns to a reddish brown. (8) Each fruit holds more than 100 cocoa beans.

(9) Twice a year, workers cut the fruits. (10) They cut them from the trees. (11) They split open the fruits and remove the beans. (12) Cocoa beans are then fermented and dried. (13) Later, the beans will be roasted and the shells removed. (14) Cocoa butter and other products will be made from the beans. (15) These products will be mixed with other ingredients to make chocolate.

GO ON →

22 How can sentences 3 and 4 **best** be combined?

Ⓐ Next to the trunk, the fruits are heavy and they grow.

Ⓑ The fruits are heavy and they grow next to the trunk.

Ⓒ The fruits are heavy, they grow next to the trunk.

Ⓓ The heavy fruits grow next to the trunk.

23 How can sentences 6 and 7 **best** be combined?

Ⓐ The fruit's hard shell turns from green to yellow and then to a reddish brown.

Ⓑ The fruit's hard shell turns from green to yellow, and it turns to a reddish brown.

Ⓒ When the fruit's hard shell turns from green to yellow, it turns to a reddish brown.

Ⓓ The fruit's hard shell turns from green to yellow, and then the shell turns to a reddish brown.

24 How can sentences 9 and 10 **best** be combined?

Ⓐ Twice a year, workers cut the fruits and cut them from the trees.

Ⓑ Twice a year, workers cut them from the trees the fruits.

Ⓒ Twice a year, workers cut the fruits from the trees.

Ⓓ Workers cut the fruits, and twice a year cut them from the trees.

25 In sentence 13, which word would **best** modify "removed"?

Ⓐ carefree

Ⓑ careful

Ⓒ carefully

Ⓓ carefulness

Literary Analysis Task

Today you will read the play "Class Project" and the story "Doreen's Dad." As you read these texts, pay attention to the central ideas to help prepare you to write an essay about a theme in each text.

Read the play "Class Project." Then answer questions 1 through 3.

Class Project

Curtain opens on ROSE's living room. JULIO, FRANK, and SOPHIE are sitting on the couch, talking over one another loudly, and laughing. ARA, sitting cross-legged on the floor, is looking at her laptop computer. ROSE, in an armchair, and BLAKE, in a folding chair, look at each other with exasperation. The coffee table is littered with the remnants of a finished snack.

JULIO: Hey! Are we done yet?

JULIO, FRANK, and SOPHIE laugh.

ROSE: Come on, everybody! (*She stands.*) This is the second time we've wasted a whole meeting. We're never going to finish this project.

SOPHIE: You mean, the Worst Project Ever?

BLAKE: I don't know about anyone else, but I am *not* getting an F in social studies. Can we at least develop a plan and assign some tasks?

SOPHIE: (*standing and mocking a teacher*) "Heritage." (*She makes air-quote gesture.*) What does that mean, anyway?

FRANK: Yeah. No one here has the same heritage. My grandparents are from Italy . . . Julio's from Mexico . . . Ara is from Afghanistan. We're all from somewhere else.

ROSE: I think that's kind of the point. But for this project, we're all in the same boat. We should talk about our different traditions, what's important, make comparisons . . . *you* know.

ARA: Rose is right. Let's go around the room and each take a turn.

BLAKE: (*grabbing a pad of paper and pen and sitting down*) I'll take notes.

JULIO: (*jumping up*) I'll start! Here's what's important to me: Baseball tryouts are tomorrow, people! (*grabs an imaginary bat and pantomimes standing at home plate*) Check out this batting stance. Bases loaded, two out in the ninth: Put one over the plate, Frankie!

GO ON →

FRANK: (*Jumps up, rips the top page from BLAKE's notepad, crumples it into a ball, winds up, and throws a pitch. JULIO swings.*) Stee-RIKE one!

BLAKE: (*standing and throwing pad of paper down in disgust*) This is ridiculous! We've got less than a week to finish this project—so, let's get the ball rolling.

ARA: (*standing with her laptop*) I'll go first. Since our last meeting, I put together this slide show. It's not much, but . . .

ROSE: It's a start. Show us.

ARA puts her laptop on the coffee table and everyone gathers around in front of it. The lights dim as the kids settle. A screen lowers from above so the audience can view the slide show.

ARA: (*narrating each slide*) This is my cousin Fila. (*Slide 1 shows a smiling Afghani girl, about eight years old, standing in front of a typical rural home.*) This year, she was excited because people in her village organized a school for girls. (*Clicks forward to Slide 2, which shows Fila and a group of other girls playing outside.*) In Afghanistan, some people don't think girls should go to school. That's why my parents brought me here to the United States. (*Clicks forward to Slide 3, which shows a young Afghani woman standing next to an easel.*) This is Fila's teacher. She helped set up this classroom in the basement of a factory. (*Clicks forward to Slide 4: Fila and other girls sitting at long tables topped with sewing machines.*) Fila says she loves going to school. The work is hard, but she knows that without an education, her future will be limited. But sometimes, classrooms like these are shut down. Fila's school was suddenly closed with no explanation. But people are organizing even more girls' schools. Fila now has a new classroom.

The screen goes dark and rises. The lights go up on the kids in the same positions around the laptop, but leaning forward, as if they have been paying close attention. All are silent and thoughtful.

JULIO: (*leaning back*) Wow.

FRANK: Thanks, Ara—seriously.

SOPHIE: You know, that gives me an idea. I don't have a slide show, or anything, but . . .

JULIO: That's okay. Let's hear it. Hey Blake, can I have some paper? I want to take some notes.

FRANK: Okay, let's focus! This project is due next week.

The lights dim as the kids put out notebooks and settle down to work. SOPHIE stands and begins talking as curtain closes.

GO ON →

1 **Part A**

Read the sentence from "Class Project."

> We've got less than a week to finish this project—so, let's get the ball rolling.

What does the phrase **get the ball rolling** suggest about Blake's plan of action?

(A) Frank should stop using his notepad as a ball.

(B) If everyone jumps in, they will find the best idea.

(C) Julio should stop pretending to play ball in the meeting.

(D) One person should start, encouraging others to follow.

Part B

Which line from the play **best** supports the answer to Part A?

(A) "We should talk about our different traditions, what's important, make comparisons . . . *you* know."

(B) "Here's what's important to me: Baseball tryouts are tomorrow, people!"

(C) "I'll go first. Since our last meeting, I put together this slide show."

(D) "This year, she was excited because people in her village organized a school for girls."

GO ON →

2 Part A

How are the first five lines of dialogue important to the plot of the play?

(A) They increase the tension.

(B) They illustrate a major lesson.

(C) They establish the conflict.

(D) They introduce the main character.

Part B

Which detail from the play **best** supports the answer to Part A?

(A) "Hey! Are we done yet?"

(B) "(*She stands.*) This is the second time we've wasted a whole meeting."

(C) "You mean, the Worst Project Ever?"

(D) "'Heritage.' (*She makes air-quote gesture.*) What does that mean, anyway?"

3 Part A

How does Ara's slide show affect the rest of the group?

(A) It inspires others to contribute their own ideas.

(B) It makes others feel ashamed for joking around.

(C) It prompts others to panic about the project deadline.

(D) It makes others worry about whether they have good ideas.

Part B

Which line from the play **best** supports the answer to Part A?

(A) "We're never going to finish this project."

(B) "I don't know about anyone else, but I am *not* getting an F in social studies."

(C) "But for this project, we're all in the same boat."

(D) "You know, that gives me an idea."

GO ON →

Read the story "Doreen's Dad." Then answer questions 4 and 5.

Doreen's Dad

1   When the school bus stopped at Doreen's corner, she grabbed her sister Addy's hand and they walked one block to their apartment.

2   "I hope Jill's already there," said Addy, excitement brightening her seven-year-old face.

3   "Of course she is, silly head," said Doreen, "because Dad left on his business trip this morning." And not a moment too soon, she noted to herself. She loved her dad, but they'd been arguing a lot lately. He was always pestering her to do her homework, or get off the phone, or help Addy get dressed, or about a million other things. He was the same as always, but she'd be in high school next year—so maybe she was just experiencing her dad in a different way. Whatever—he was off at a writer's conference for three days, and Doreen was looking forward to the break.

4   The minute Doreen opened the apartment door, Addy dumped her backpack on the floor and ran to look for Jill. A recent college graduate, Jill was their regular babysitter, but this was the first time she'd ever looked after them during the school week.

5   Doreen wandered into the kitchen for a snack. Her dad, a writer, worked at home, and usually had something delicious ready for the girls after school. Today the table was empty.

6   "Look who I found in Dad's office," said Addy, dragging Jill by the hand.

7   Jill smiled at Doreen and gave her a big hug. "Addy caught me in the act of working on my grad school applications."

8   "Yuck," said Doreen, opening the refrigerator and perusing its contents. Grabbing a wedge of cheese and some apples, she carried them to the cutting board. Then her phone rang, and Doreen went into her room to talk to her friend Marie. Afterwards, she found Jill and Addy in the living room, playing a game. The snack food still sat on the cutting board where she'd left it, so Doreen got to work cutting everything up.

GO ON →

9 A few hours later, Doreen helped Jill make spaghetti. Whenever Dad cooked dinner, all the pieces seemed to come together at the same time. Tonight, however, things were chaotic. By the time Jill drained the pasta, the salad had yet to be made. When everything was finally ready, they realized the table hadn't been set. The salad tasted fine, but the spaghetti was all mushy. And now, it was almost past Addy's bedtime—so Doreen had to clean everything up by herself while Jill read Addy a story.

10 When Addy was asleep, Jill asked Doreen if she'd done her homework. "Almost," she said, though she hadn't even started it, taking advantage of her dad's absence to just laze around until dinner.

11 After staying up late to finish her homework, Doreen dragged herself out of bed the next morning to find Jill arguing with Addy over wearing her tutu to school. Doreen sighed, dragging out cereal, bowls, and milk. She reminisced about Dad's scrambled eggs and waffles as she slurped her oat flakes and dreamed of a hot breakfast.

12 It was almost time to head down to the bus stop when Jill started taking sandwich fixings from the refrigerator.

13 "Dad always packs our lunches the night before—there's no time to do it now!"

14 Jill gave them lunch money, and, grabbing Addy's hand, Doreen hustled her out the door. On the bus, Doreen considered the fact that until this trip, she never realized how well Dad had everything organized. When he got home, she should tell him what a good dad he was. Well, it was something to think about, anyway.

GO ON →

4 **Part A**

What does the word **reminisced** mean as it is used in paragraph 11 of "Doreen's Dad"?

(A) recalled

(B) renewed

(C) prepared

(D) preferred

Part B

Which word from paragraph 11 is a clue to the meaning of **reminisced** in Part A?

(A) finish

(B) arguing

(C) slurped

(D) dreamed

GO ON →

5 Which sentences would be important to include in a summary of "Doreen's Dad"? Select **four** details from the list below, and write them in the chart in chronological order.

Summary	
1	
2	
3	
4	

Details:

Doreen receives a phone call from Marie.

Doreen has a disorganized afternoon and a hurried morning.

Jill drains the pasta before making salad.

Doreen looks forward to having a babysitter.

Dad's absence helps Doreen appreciate him.

Addy and Jill play a game in the living room.

Jill works on her school applications.

Doreen misses Dad's after-school snack.

GO ON →

Name: _____ Date: _____

Refer to the play "Class Project" and the story "Doreen's Dad." Then answer questions 6 and 7.

6 Read the central ideas in the list and decide whether they are found in the drama "Class Project" or the story "Doreen's Dad." Write **each** central idea in the chart.

"Class Project"	"Doreen's Dad"

Central Ideas

Being a parent is much harder than it looks.

One great idea can lead to another.

Learning about our backgrounds can bring people together.

People often appreciate something most when it is absent.

GO ON →

7 You have read the play "Class Project" and the story "Doreen's Dad." Think about the similarities and differences in how the authors develop the themes in each text.

Write an essay that identifies a theme from each text and explains how each theme is expressed. Be sure to support your response with evidence from **both** texts.

Write your essay on a separate sheet of paper.

STOP

Name: _____

Question	Correct Answer	Content Focus	CCSS	Complexity
1A	A	Latin Roots	RI.6.1, RI.6.4, L.6.4b	DOK 1
1B	A	Latin Roots	RI.6.1, RI.6.4, L.6.4b	DOK 1
2A	C	Greek Roots	RI.6.1, RI.6.4, L.6.4b	DOK 1
2B	B	Greek Roots	RI.6.1, RI.6.4, L.6.4b	DOK 2
3	see below	Text Structure: Sequence	RI.6.1, RI.6.5	DOK 2
4	see below	Text Structure: Cause and Effect	RI.6.1, RI.6.3	DOK 2
5A	B	Main Idea and Key Details	RI.6.1, RI.6.2	DOK 2
5B	D	Main Idea and Key Details	RI.6.1, RI.6.2	DOK 2
6A	D	Context Clues: Comparisons	RI.6.1, RI.6.4, L.6.5b	DOK 2
6B	E, F	Context Clues: Comparisons	RI.6.1, RI.6.4, L.6.5b	DOK 2
7	C	Adages and Proverbs	RI.6.1, RI.6.4, L.6.5a	DOK 2
8	C	Text Structure: Cause and Effect	RI.6.1, RI.6.3	DOK 2
9A	B	Text Structure: Cause and Effect	RI.6.1, RI.6.3	DOK 2
9B	D	Text Structure: Cause and Effect	RI.6.1, RI.6.3	DOK 2
10	see below	Text Structure: Sequence	RI.6.1, RI.6.5	DOK 2
11A	C	Main Idea and Key Details	RI.6.1, RI.6.2	DOK 2
11B	D	Main Idea and Key Details	RI.6.1, RI.6.2	DOK 2
12	see below	Text Structure: Cause and Effect	RI.6.1, RI.6.3	DOK 3
13	B	Hyperbole	RL.6.1, RL.6.4, L.6.5a	DOK 2
14A	B	Theme	RL.6.1, RL.6.2	DOK 3
14B	A, F	Theme	RL.6.1, RL.6.2	DOK 2
15	see below	Compare Across Texts	W.6.9	DOK 4
16	C	Adverbs	L.6.1	DOK 1
17	B	Negatives	L.6.1	DOK 1
18	A	Adverbs that Compare	L.6.1	DOK 1

Answer Key

Question	Correct Answer	Content Focus	CCSS	Complexity
19	C	Prepositional Phrases	L.6.1	DOK 1
20	B	Adverbs that Compare	L.6.1	DOK 1
21	A	Negatives	L.6.1	DOK 1
22	D	Sentence Combining	L.6.2	DOK 1
23	A	Sentence Combining	L.6.2	DOK 1
24	C	Prepositional Phrases	L.6.1	DOK 1
25	C	Adverbs	L.6.1	DOK 1

Comprehension: Selected Response 3, 4, 5A, 5B, 8, 9A, 9B, 11A, 11B, 12, 14A, 14B	/16	%
Comprehension: Constructed Response 10, 15	/6	%
Vocabulary 1A, 1B, 2A, 2B, 6A, 6B, 7, 13	/10	%
Grammar, Mechanics, Usage 16–25	/10	%
Total Unit Assessment Score	/42	%

3 Students should write the following numbers next to the steps: 5, 1, 2, 4, 3.

4 Students should draw lines to match each technique to its effect:
- putting the bonsai in a shallow clay pot—keeps the tree small
- wrapping the trunk and branches in copper wire—forms a variety of shapes and styles
- scarring the branches and trunk so they die and turn gray—makes the tree more appealing
- harvesting a bonsai from its natural setting—carries a risk that the tree will die

10 Students should write the following numbers next to the events: 4, 3, 1, 5, 2.

12 **2-point response:** The author organizes the text using cause and effect to describe the positive and negative impacts that a new port for coal in Cherry Point would have. A positive effect of building the gateway is that it would create jobs. However, it would damage the environment. The author describes both sides of the situation to provide examples of what will be discussed when the decision is made.

15 **4-point response:** Both texts express the idea that damage to the environment has global impact. The author of "The Uncertain Fate of the Gateway Pacific Coal Terminal" presents a situation that greatly affects the quality of the environment. The building of the terminal is described as bringing a lot of pollution and other threats to the environment. While the author seems to present a neutral opinion about the fate of the terminal, the author provides evidence to suggest that the environment needs greater protection. The author quotes an environmentalist to show that burning fossil fuels at the terminal can lead cause climate change. The author also mentions renewable energy sources like water, wind, and solar power as possible substitutes for burning coal.

One of the most important facts about the terminal is that it has not been built yet; the final decision is still being figured out by all kinds of business people and government agencies. This factor speaks directly to the repeated stanza of the poem, where the most important line is "The time to act is now at hand." The speaker of the poem, a polar bear, stresses how we need to act quickly, "while we still have icy land" (line 35). The fate of humans and animals depends on it.

Name: _____

		Unit 6 Assessment: Literary Analysis Task		
Question	**Answer**	**CCSS**		**Complexity**
1A	D	RL.6.1, RL.6.4, L.6.5a		DOK 2
1B	C			DOK 2
2A	C	RL.6.1, RL.6.5		DOK 3
2B	B			DOK 2
3A	A	RL.6.1, RL.6.3		DOK 2
3B	D			DOK 2
4A	A	RL.6.1, RL.6.4		DOK 2
4B	D			DOK 2
5	see below	RL.6.1, RL.6.2		DOK 3
6	see below	RL.6.1, RL.6.2		DOK 3
7	see below	RL.6.1, RL.6.2 W.6.1, W.6.2, W.6.4–W.6.10 L.6.1, L.6.2, L.6.3, L.6.6		DOK 4

Comprehension 2A, 2B, 3A, 3B, 5, 6		/8	%
Vocabulary 1A, 1B, 4A, 4B		/4	%
Prose Constructed Response 7		/4 [RC] /12 [WE] /3 [LC]	%
Total Literary Analysis Score		/31	%

5 Students should write the following details in the chart:
  1: Doreen looks forward to having a babysitter.
  2: Doreen misses Dad's after-school snack.
  3: Doreen has a disorganized afternoon and a hurried morning.
  4: Dad's absence helps Doreen appreciate him.

6 Students should write the central ideas in the chart as follows:
  • "Class Project"—"One great idea can lead to another," "Learning about our backgrounds can bring people together."
  • "Doreen's Dad"—"Being a parent is much harder than it looks," "People often appreciate something most when it is absent."

7 **19-point anchor paper:**

Both "Class Project" and "Doreen's Dad" involve characters who learn to respect or appreciate others. However, each text expresses a different specific theme and uses a different narrative structure to convey these ideas.

"Class Project" is a drama about a group of six students who are assigned to work on a "Heritage" project. The major theme expressed in the play is, "One good example can inspire many great ideas." As the play begins, about half the students goof off, and the other half are upset that, as the deadline approaches, they haven't made any progress. One character, Sophie, calls their assignment "the Worst Project Ever." But when Blake begs everyone to get to work, we realize that Sophie's frustration comes not just from a lack of willpower. She doesn't really understand the project: "'Heritage.' (She makes air-quote gesture.) What does that mean, anyway?" Then Frank chimes in to note that "We're all from somewhere else," listing Italy, Mexico, and Afghanistan.

Through the stage directions and the characters' dialogue, the students continue to struggle with the idea. After one more diversion in which Julio and Frank pretend to play baseball, Blake gets even more frustrated. This prompts Ara, who's been mostly silent so far, to show a slide show she developed after their last meeting.

The audience and the reader see the presentation through Ara's words, as well as stage directions that describe each slide. Everyone watches with great interest, touched by the subject matter (her cousin and other girls fight to go to school in Afghanistan). Right after the slide show ends, Sophie says, "You know, that gives me an idea." As the play ends, the kids are all engaged in the subject matter and seem eager to contribute. So, through watching one group of kids struggle with how to approach a topic, the theme about one example sparking other ideas comes through.

"Doreen's Dad" is a story about a girl who is looking forward to her dad going away on business. The major theme in the story is, "You don't really don't appreciate something until it's gone." Doreen loves her dad, but as she notes in paragraph 3: "He was always pestering her to do her homework, or get off the phone, or help Addy get dressed, or about a million other things." So Doreen is feeling the need for more independence, and is glad that she can do things differently now that her dad is away. The reader understands Doreen mostly through the narration, which presents her thoughts and feelings.

Right away, Doreen feels her dad's absence—and not in the way she expected. There's no snack ready after school, and Doreen has to make it herself. She's glad that Jill doesn't nag her about homework, so she puts it off. Then, when she helps Jill with dinner, she realizes how organized Dad was, with everything ready at the same time and the table set. But that's not what happens tonight. And when things runs late, Doreen has to clean up all by herself so Jill can put Addy to bed. The author develops the theme through these events, as Doreen realizes that what she experiences as annoying routines are actually important ways Dad cares for the family and keeps things running smoothly. This point is emphasized when Doreen realizes she forgot to do her homework, and then the next morning, when lunches aren't made in time to catch the bus.

In case the lesson isn't clear, it's summed up at the end: "On the bus ride, Doreen considered the fact that until this trip, she never realized how well Dad had everything organized. When he got home, she should tell him what a good dad he was. Well, it was something to think about, anyway."